Trinity Sunday

Revisited

TRINITY SUNDAY REVISITED

PATTERNS FOR PRAYER

Robert F. Morneau

THE LITURGICAL PRESS

Collegeville   Minnesota

Library of Congress Cataloging in Publication Data

Morneau, Robert F   1938–
    Trinity Sunday revisited.

    Includes bibliographical references.
    1.   Devotional exercises. 2.   Prayer. 3.   Herbert,
George, 1593–1633. I.   Title.
BX2182.2.M67   242   79-25097
ISBN 0-8146-1084-6

English translation of excerpts from the Roman Missal, the Liturgy of the Hours, the Rite of Penance, and the Rite of Christian Initiation of Adults, copyright © 1969, 1970, 1972, 1973, 1974, 1975, 1978 by the International Committee on English in the Liturgy, Inc. All rights reserved.

Excerpts from the Jerusalem Bible, copyright © 1966, 1967, 1968 by Darton, Longman & Todd Ltd. and Doubleday & Company, Inc. Used by permission.

The section entitled "Principles of Prayer" was published in *Review for Religious*, May, 1979, and is reprinted with the permission of the publisher.

Nihil obstat: Joseph C. Kremer, S.T.L., *Censor deputatus. Imprimatur:* ✝George H. Speltz, D.D., Bishop of St. Cloud. September 4, 1979.
    Printed in the United States of America.

CONTENTS

Trinity Sunday
Revisited

INTRODUCTION

Our pilgrimage to the Father is enriched by various companions who are sent to share in our journey and point out the way. Dante was aided by Virgil, Plato by Socrates, Timothy by Paul. Because of their dialogue, the journey took on an added richness and joy.

George Herbert, a metaphysical poet of the early seventeenth century, has guided many people to the Father by means of his faith-poetry. In incisive verse, this man of God captured many profound movements of the way God works within the human heart. One of his poems that has touched my own life is entitled "Trinity Sunday."

> Lord, who has form'd me out of mud,
> And has redeem'd me through thy blood,
> And sanctifi'd me to do good;
>
> Purge all my sins done heretofore:
> For I confess my heavy score,
> And I will strive to sin no more.
>
> Enrich my heart, mouth, hands in me,
> With faith, with hope, with charity;
> That I may run, rise, rest with thee.

This poem is used as a skeletal structure for these notes on prayer. From the three stanzas, some thirty-two themes are identified for quiet reflection. By relating each hour of prayer back to the entire poem, a sense of unity can be felt and nourished.

An example of themes can be taken from the first line: "Lord, who has form'd me out of mud." Addressing the Lord as "Lord" takes us into the area of *prayer*; "being formed" speaks of *creation*; "out of mud" tells of *humanness* and *humility*. Thus we can ponder in depth our communication with God, the realization that we are creatures, the joys and pains of being human, and the invitation to live in the truth of who we are.

Methodology

Because of the highly personal character of prayer, the methodology contained in these notes should be used with great flexibility. The method begins with a theme and desire, the first helping us to focus on a single subject of prayer, and the second helping us to prepare our hearts for the Lord's working. An introductory verse follows, allowing us to "ease" into prayer with a sense of reverence and awe. The central portion of the prayer time contains three "points," the first two taken from God's word, and the third selected from the liturgy or the office. A concluding selection helps us to summarize our prayer time.

A method is a means to an end. The end of prayer is union with God. Thus, if any single verse puts us into the presence of God, we let the rest go. It is not necessary nor advisable to cover all the material given in each hour of prayer; rather, we are to taste and savor what is given, never moving on when being nourished.

Prayer experiences can be aided through the understanding of some universal patterns that underlie communication between God and his human creature. The following principles are offered as a guide to enrich those moments when we "go apart to rest awhile" in his presence.

Principles of Prayer

Growth in all forms of relationships, be they with God or with one another, calls for an ongoing communication process. Prayer is one such process involving dialogue between God and the human person. In order to be meaningful, that process must be grounded on certain principles descriptive of universal conditions, consequences, and causes of meaningful prayer.

Here we want to cull out several principles of prayer as articulated by various spiritual authors. These people, experiencing prayer at different levels according to the uniqueness of their personality structures, share in written form some truths that provide meaning and explication of prayer experiences in general. These truths, when understood in context, may well enlighten our own experiences or at least cause us to desire them as we journey to the Father. In so doing we can grow in our dialogical relationship with God.

A three-step method will be used: (1) a statement of a principle of prayer; (2) a series of quotations from which the principle was drawn or quotations used to demonstrate the validity of the principle; (3) a commentary developing some implications buried within the principle and/or quotations.

Though principles are significant and advantageous in providing a perspective and pointing out a direction, experience itself is the central concern. It is hoped that as the reader journeys beyond the principle into the experience that it elucidates, he or she will find deeper meaning in it and be able to come into contact with the principal Reality underlying all real principles.

TEN PRINCIPLES OF PRAYER

1. Prayer is essentially loving attention.[1]

Thus the individual also should proceed only with a loving attention to God, without making specific acts. He should conduct himself passively, as we have said, without efforts of his own, but with the simple, loving awareness, as a person who opens his eyes with loving attention.[2]

Attention animated by desire is the whole foundation of religious practices.[3]

I shall not dwell upon this because I want to say something about the way in which I think those of us who practice prayer may profit, though everything is profitable to a soul that loves the Lord with fervent desire, since it instills into it courage and wonder.[4]

Two essential elements of authentic prayer are contained in the definition of prayer as loving attention: awareness of the presence of the Other and a heartfelt, concerned response. Distraction within consciousness and indifference of the heart block meaningful communication with God. If, on our part, we are called to love with attention, this is consequent upon God's loving attention toward us. God made us; he is attentive to the smallest detail of our lives; he loves us completely. An affirmative answer must be given to Blake's deeply religious question: "Did he smile his work to see?"

1. See Jn. 17; Rom. 11:33–36.

2. *The Collected Works of St. John of the Cross*, trans. Kieran Kavanaugh, O.C.D., and Otilio Rodriguez, O.C.D. (Washington, D.C.: ICS Publications, 1973), p. 622.

3. Simone Weil, *Waiting for God* (New York: Harper Colophon Books, 1951), p. 197.

4. *The Complete Works of St. Theresa of Jesus*, ed. and trans. E. Allison Peers (London: Sheed & Ward, 1944), 2:363.

The Father's loving attention has been revealed in Jesus, the Word incarnate. A coming-to-visit verifies God's love and awareness. Further verification is found in the sending of the Spirit into our lives, the Spirit of love and knowledge. Because of this personal Grace we are enabled to truly pray:

> The Spirit too comes to help us in our weakness. For when we cannot choose words in order to pray properly, the Spirit himself expresses our plea in a way that could never be put into words, and God who knows everything in our hearts knows perfectly well what he means, and that the pleas of the saints expressed by the Spirit are according to the mind of God.[5]

Defining prayer in terms of loving attention is simple but not simplistic. Its simplicity lies in its directness and succinctness; it is not reductionistic, because neither love nor attentiveness is easily attained. Prayer, like all great acts, defies full analysis, because it contains too much mystery. Only knowledge of prayer from the inside, that is, through experience, allows for even surface knowledge of such a powerful event.

2. Prayer is proportionate to the quality of one's love.[6]

> Farewell, farewell! but this I tell
> To thee, thou Wedding-Guest!
> He prayeth well, who loveth well
> Both man and bird and beast.
>
> He prayeth best, who loveth best
> All things both great and small;
> For the dear God who loveth us,
> He made and loveth all.[7]

He knew that without prayer true love was impossible, and he learned from living that without love prayer became self-centered and barren.[8]

I repeat that if you have this in view you must not build upon foundations of prayer and contemplation alone, for, unless you strive after the virtues and practice them, you will never grow to be more than dwarfs. God grant that nothing worse than this

5. Rom. 8:26-27.
6. 1 Jn. 2:9-11; Lk. 4:42-44.
7. Samuel Taylor Coleridge, "The Rime of the Ancient Mariner."
8. Murray Bodo, *Francis: The Journey and the Dream* (Cincinnati: St. Anthony Messenger Press, 1972), p. 64.

may happen — for, as you know, anyone who fails to go forward begins to go back, and love, I believe, can never be content to stay for long where it is.[9]

The spiritual life demands balance. How one relates to God in prayer is intimately related to how one encounters his neighbor. Scripture is transparent on this point: one who says that he or she loves God and at the same time shows hatred to his or her neighbor is a liar.[10] The person who spends an hour in prayer while neglecting the obvious needs of people close at hand must seriously examine the authenticity of such prayer. Indeed, the touchstone for one's prayer life is fraternal charity.[11]

Prayer and love are symbiotic. Since our God is Love, we must be in close contact with him if we are to share that gift with others to its fullest. The reverse is also true: unless we share the love given in prayer, the gift dries up or simply engenders pride. As in all provinces of life, the principle of interdependence applies directly to the spiritual life, too. Integration of prayer and love, contemplation and virtue, liturgy and the apostolate are called for. Isolation and fragmentation here create a false spirituality visible to everyone except their possessor. A vision of integrated spirituality and a discipline of courageous action is true imitation of Christ.

3. Genuine prayer demands some self-control of body and spirit.[12]

. . . we shall not fail to observe the fasts, disciplines and periods of silence which the order commands; for, as you know, if prayer is to be genuine it must be reinforced with these things — prayer cannot be accompanied by self-indulgence.[13]

Oh, who can tell how impossible it is for a man with appetites to judge the things of God as they are?[14]

We shall have overcome a considerable obstacle when prayer and penance condition each other, for their unity will be able to become the guarantee of their orientation. If it is necessary to deprive oneself of food and sleep, it is not to establish a perform-

---

9. *The Complete Works of St. Theresa of Jesus*, 2:347.
10. 1 Jn. 2.
11. *Spiritual Renewal of the American Priesthood* (Washington, D.C.: Publications Office, United States Catholic Conference, 1973), p. 48.
12. Gal. 5:16–26; Mt. 4:1–17.
13. *The Complete Works of St. Theresa of Jesus*, 2:16.
14. *The Collected Works of St. John of the Cross*, p. 364.

ance or glorify oneself over an exploit, but to allow the spirit to give itself freely to prayer, since, if it is less strongly captivated by the things of earth, it will be able to give attention to what is above it.[15]

When the body or the spirit is not free but addicted to various substances or objects, the process of prayer is threatened. A body satiated with food and drink becomes listless and weary; a mind constantly filled with the flood of stimuli is so preoccupied as not to be receptive to other realities. Prayer is premised upon the ability to say no to one level of reality so as to be able to say yes to the workings of the Holy Spirit.

Asceticism is a condition that creates space and time for dialogue with God. Certain exercises, such as fasting, periods of extended silence, or voluntary mortification, are means by which that space and time become real. The "if-then principle" applies to spirituality as it does to all of life: if the farmer wants the fall harvest, then he must willingly do the spring plowing and planting; if a person wants to listen and respond to the Lord, then the time and space must be created for the encounter to happen. Strong and determined desire lies at the root of such discipline.

Self-control extends one step beyond asceticism. Once the emptiness has been created through exercises done out of love, the soul must wait on the Lord, who will come in his own time and in his own manner. Waiting for God is at the heart of prayer and is already a deep form of prayer; self-control makes that waiting possible, and grace makes it sacred. Although not speaking of prayer, C. S. Lewis describes well an aspect of the human condition: "Then came the worst part, the waiting."[16]

4. In prayer, I must bring this me to the living and true God.[17]

I enter into the presence of God with all my load of misery and troubles. And he takes me just as I am and makes me to be alone with Him.[18]

15. Francois Roustang, S.J., *Growth in the Spirit*, trans. Kathleen Pond (New York: Sheed & Ward, 1966), p. 232.

16. C. S. Lewis, *The Last Battle* (New York: Collier Books, 1956), p. 13.

17. Jg. 6:13; Rom. 7:14–25. This principle of prayer was presented in a guided retreat by Fr. William A. M. Peters, S.J.

18. *Raïssa's Journal*, presented by Jacques Maritain (Albany, N.Y.: Magi Books, 1963), p. 225.

If you're approaching Him not as the goal but as a road, not as the end but as a means, you're not really approaching Him at all.[19]

I can testify that this is one of the most grievous kinds of life which I think can be imagined, for I had neither any joy in God nor any pleasure in the world. When I was in the midst of worldly pleasures, I was distressed by the remembrance of what I owed to God; when I was with God, I grew restless because of worldly affections.[20]

Any genuine conversation requires that each participant have an adequate level of self-knowledge and be familiar with the content under discussion. Where either is wanting, communication breaks down. Prayer, which is essentially a form of communication, requires the same: we must know our real self and have some notion of who God is as well as understand the experience being shared. Because we always want to come off looking good, it is difficult to bring our real, true self to God without editing. Because God can be conceived in ways that are distortions of his true nature, it can easily happen that we attempt to pray to gods that do not exist. One of the greatest causes of sterility in prayer is a misconception of God and a failure to be in touch with our true identity.

Psychologists are helpful in depicting for us a variety of selves with which we must deal:

Each of us seems to have three *self-concepts.* The *personal* self-image is how the individual pictures his most inner self ("how I really am"). The *social* self is how he thinks others see him, and the pattern of responses he learns in order to be a social being. The *ideal* self is made up of the goals set by parents, the culture, and other sources ("how I *should* be"). Often, these three conflict, creating problems for the individual trying to satisfy them all.[21]

Each person must examine which of these selves is operative not only in the interactions of one's daily life but also as one comes before God. To play a role in the presence of the Lord prohibits encounter with our deepest self. To demand that our ideal self (perfectionism) be actual-

19. C. S. Lewis, *Surprised by Joy* (New York: Harcourt, Brace & World, 1955), p. 21.

20. *The Complete Works of St. Theresa of Jesus,* 1:48.

21. John H. Brennecke and Robert G. Amick, *Psychology: Understanding Yourself* (Beverly Hills, Calif.: Benziger, Bruce & Glencoe, 1975), p. 43.

ized before we pray only leads to a guilt trip. God says to us, "Come as you are—no need for formal dress here."

C. S. Lewis knew that God cannot be captured by our finite reason: "My idea of God is not a divine idea. It has to be shattered time after time."[22] Yet we can come to some knowledge of the living and true God. As Christians we attain to this through faith and knowledge of Jesus Christ. In Jesus, our God is made visible. Gifted with the Spirit, we make our journey to the Father in and through Jesus. His life, death, and resurrection are a summary statement of the Father's love and forgiveness. Thus all of our prayer passes through, and is enriched by, Jesus as we speak to and listen to the Father.

Authentic prayer demands authentic persons. Our real self must be continually searched out; our real God must be longed for and awaited in silence and solitude. Only when real people meet can dialogue take place. The dialogue of prayer is no exception.

5. Prayer's primary focus is on God, not on self or on events.[23]

I get nowhere by looking at myself; I merely get discouraged. So I am making the resolution to abandon myself entirely to God, to look only at him, to leave all the care of myself to him, to practice only one thing, *confidence*; my extreme wretchedness, my natural cowardice leaving me no other way to go to God and to advance in good.[24]

It is not my business to think about myself. My business is to think about God. It is for God to think about me.[25]

You could, if you wished, deny that Mister God existed, but then any denial didn't alter the fact that Mister God was. No, Mister God was; he *was* the kingpin, the center, the very heart of things; and this is where it got funny. You see, we had to recognize that he was all these things, and that meant that we were at our center, not God. God is our center, and yet it is we who acknowledge that he is the center. That makes us somehow internal to Mister God. This is the curious nature of Mister God: that even while he is at the center of all things, he waits outside us and knocks to come in. It is we who open the door. Mister

22. C. S. Lewis, *A Grief Observed* (New York: Seabury Press, 1961), p. 52.
23. Ps. 23; Gal. 2:17-21.
24. *Raïssa's Journal*, p. 83.
25. Simone Weil, pp. 50-51.

God doesn't break it down and come in; no, he knocks and waits.[26]

Focusing and centering are concepts and experiences that are emphasized in spirituality and psychology. Through this activity we realize that what is at the core of our consciousness radically affects our thoughts, feelings, and actions. Often a violent struggle takes place in the deepest part of our being as various persons, forces, and things vie for centrality.

Prayer deals directly with centering. Our experience indicates how easily self-centeredness moves in or how daily anxieties and worries can become so strong as to exclude any awareness of a loving, caring God. Self-transcendence is no easy task; trust that the Lord will provide is more easily thought than experienced. Only in grace can the obstacles blocking our encounter with God be removed. Jesus' prayer and life were centered on the Father and the doing of his will. Often in the early hours and before major events, Jesus explicitly turned to the Father in deep, familiar communication. These explicit moments were indications of an implicit, hidden life of union. How else explain the intimacy of the Last Supper discourse? Yet Jesus, in his humanness, must have struggled at times to keep proper focus. We need but ponder his agony in the garden to realize that the struggle we have with ourselves and our fear of suffering were part of Jesus' experience as well.

The lives of the saints are records of people who struggled to center on God in spite of their own selfishness. Augustine's ongoing conversion, Teresa of Avila's admission that for years her prayer was superficial, John of the Cross' constant challenge to mortification lest the self dominate—all manifest the eternal conflict between the ego and divine love. Marvelously God withholds rest so that we can never be fully at peace unless we center on him. George Herbert saw this and recorded it magnificently:

> When God at first made man,
> Having a glass of blessings standing by,
> Let us (said he) pour on him all we can;
> Let the world's riches, which dispersed lie,
> Contract into a span.

26. Fynn, *Mister God, This Is Anna* (New York: Holt, Rinehart & Winston, 1974), p. 174.

So strength first made a way;
Then beauty flow'd, then wisdom, honour, pleasure:
When almost all was out, God made a stay,
Perceiving that, alone of all his treasure,
   Rest in the bottom lay.

For if I should (said he)
Bestow this jewel also on my creature,
He would adore my gifts instead of me,
And rest in Nature, not the God of Nature:
   So both should losers be.

Yet let him keep the rest,
But keep them with repining restlessness;
Let him be rich and weary, that at least,
If goodness lead him not, yet weariness
   May toss him to my breast.[27]

6. Silence, solitude, and surrender are conditions for prayer.[28]
When it happens, therefore, that a person is conscious in this
manner of being placed in solitude and in the state of listening,
he should even forget the practice of loving attentiveness I men-
tioned so as to remain free for what the Lord then desires of
him.[29]

The beginning of integrity is not effort but surrender; it is simply
the opening of the heart to receive that for which the heart is
longing. The healing of mankind begins whenever any man
ceases to resist the love of God.[30]

Good as is discourse, silence is better, and shames it. The length
of the discourse indicates the distance of thought betwixt the
speaker and the hearer. If they were at a perfect understanding
in any part, no words would be necessary thereon. If at one in
all parts, no words would be suffered.[31]

This SSS principle (Silence, Solitude, Surrender) establishes the dis-
positions allowing for union with God. Simply by looking at their op-
posites we realize how important they are. Constant chatter impedes

27. George Herbert, "The Pulley."
28. Lk. 22:39–46; Mt. 6:5–6.
29. *The Collected Works of St. John of the Cross,* p. 623.
30. Caryll Houselander, quoted in Maisie Ward, *Caryll Houselander: That Divine Eccentric* (New York: Sheed & Ward, 1962), p. 279.
31. "Circles," *Essays of Ralph Waldo Emerson* (New York: The Book League of America, 1941), p. 106.

prayer ("In your prayers do not babble as the pagans do"—Mt. 6:5); crowding our lives with activities and people stifles the inner agenda; clutching desperately to our own wills thwarts the realization of the Father's will.

In a culture that is activistic and grasping, silence, solitude, and surrender are not easy to come by. We must recognize the influence of the external environment on the internal milieu. Diligence and discipline are required if we are to grow in a rich, interior silence; courage and trust, if we are to dwell alone with the Other; love and generosity, if we are to accomplish the Lord's will freely.

The attainment of a given end necessitates appropriate means. The house of the Lord is attained by traveling the path of silence, solitude, and surrender. The path is narrow, perhaps peopled by few. Desire for union with God provides the enthusiasm to set out and continue on the journey. The greatest tragedy is to ignore the voices that call us to love, to dwell with many and not to have the One, to retain a false freedom at the cost of life.

7. *The tone of prayer is one of reverence and awe.*[32]

Then prayer is a witness that the soul wills as God wills, and it eases the conscience and fits man for grace. And so he teaches us to pray and to have firm trust that we shall have it; for he beholds us in love, and wants to make us partners in his good will and work.[33]

> Earth's crammed with heaven
> And every common bush afire with God;
> And only he who sees takes off his shoes —
> The rest sit round and pluck blackberries.[34]

> First, therefore, I invite the reader
> to the groans of prayer
> through Christ crucified,
> through whose blood
> we are cleansed from the filth of vice —
> so that he not believe
> that reading is sufficient without unction,

32. Is. 6:1-9; Ps. 118:5-7.
33. *Julian of Norwich: Showings,* translated from the critical text with an introduction by Edmund Colledge, O.S.A., and James Walsh, S.J. (New York: Paulist Press, 1978), p. 253.
34. Elizabeth Barrett Browning, "Aurora Leigh."

> speculation without devotion,
> investigation without wonder,
> observation without joy,
> work without piety,
> knowledge without love,
> understanding without humility,
> endeavor without divine grace,
> reflection as a mirror without divinely inspired wisdom.[35]

A personal attitude toward a particular person or object is known as tone. Hostility, lack of openness, and prejudices are negative attitudes creating an atmosphere (tone) of fear and discomfort; gentleness, respect, and affability are positive attitudes promoting a climate (tone) of warmth and joy. The interior manner by which we approach God is of great importance in prayer. Julian of Norwich writes that when one is comfortable in coming to the Lord, deeper experiences of prayer are possible:

> And so prayer makes harmony between God and man's soul, because when man is at ease with God he does not need to pray, but to contemplate reverently what God says.[36]

Though our tone is important, of greater significance is the manner in which God comes to us in prayer. God's attitude flows from his nature, a nature that is summarized in the word "love." And love's cousins are reverence and awe. What mystery here — our God is so gracious and courteous in his visitations to us! Julian of Norwich shares her experience of God's tonality:

> Of everything which I saw, this was the greatest comfort to me, that our Lord is so familiar and so courteous, and this most filled my soul with delight and surety.[37]

When we enter into prayer, it is of great profit to ask for the Spirit of reverence and awe, the same Spirit that empowered Jesus as he addressed the Father in silence and solitude. Reverence and awe are essentially gifts and are to be asked for. When we are gifted with these gentle attitudes, our prayer takes on an entirely different quality. Without these gifts our hearts are stifled and our service cool. The

---

35. *Bonaventure: The Soul's Journey into God,* trans. Ewert Cousins (New York: Paulist Press, 1978), pp. 55–56.

36. *Julian of Norwich: Showings,* p. 159.

37. *Ibid.,* p. 136

reverent feel deeply and serve generously; the awe-filled see with wonder and hear with trembling.

8. God's activity in prayer is far more important than our activity.[38]

Prayer is a personal response to God's presence. It is more something that God does to us, rather than anything we do. This means that God first makes Himself present to us. Prayer is our awareness of and then response to God.[39]

In this interior union God communicates Himself to the soul with such genuine love that no mother's affection, in which she tenderly caresses her child, nor brother's love, nor friendship is comparable to it. The tenderness and truth of love by which the immense Father favors and exalts this humble and loving soul reaches such a degree — O wonderful thing, worthy of all our awe and admiration — that the Father Himself becomes subject to her for her exaltation, as though he were her servant and she His lord. And He is as solicitous in favoring her as He would be if He were her slave and she His god. So profound is the humility and sweetness of God![40]

In the first place it should be known that if a person is seeking God, his Beloved is seeking him much more.[41]

Self-sufficiency is a trait much admired by our culture. Nothing happens unless we make it happen; being responsible implies the total management of our lives, including the spiritual domain. Control is the goal. With such a mentality, it is not surprising that God's invitations and graces fall on deaf ears and are unseen because of our blindness. We simply are not open to outside motivation; we are dancers who must always lead. The consequence of such a disposition is tragic: "A person extinguishes the spirit by wanting to conduct himself in a way different from that in which God is leading him."[42]

While acknowledging both the necessity and health of self-reliance in its deepest meaning, complete self-motivation leads to stagnation and death. Faith tells us that God always takes the initiative, that Christian life is a radical response to what God speaks and calls us to do. In no way does this deny the principle that we are challenged to

38. Ps. 138; Jn. 6:44.
39. Fr. Armand Nigro's "Prayer" (source unknown).
40. *The Collected Works of St. John of the Cross*, p. 517.
41. *Ibid.*, p. 620.
42. *Ibid.*, p. 232.

make things happen, not just let them happen. But that making is consequent upon the word of our Father. The Christian heart, in wisdom, seeks simply to please the Father, whatever is asked. Though the request may be surrounded by darkness, though his thoughts and ways differ from our own, the challenge will remain the same: "Our task is always the humble and courageous one of listening obediently and acting boldly."[43] Our activity must flow from that deep listening to the word of God. The day should begin with a listening disposition; it should end with a review of our response to the Father's word.

Thus, prayer is dialogic: a word is spoken in love and answered out of love. The answer itself becomes the substance for the next movement in the warm, mutual relationship between God and his creature. The familiarity here is profound; its absence creates an incredible loneliness and a haunting restlessness.

9. There is no one way of praying; pluralism in prayer must be carefully safeguarded.[44]

If while the soul is meditating the Lord should suspend it, well and good; for in that case He will make it cease meditation even against its own will. I consider it quite certain that this method of procedure is no hindrance to the soul but a great help to it in everything that is good; whereas, if it laboured hard at meditation in the way I have already described, this would indeed be a hindrance — in fact, I believe such labour is impossible for a person who has attained greater heights. This may not be so with everyone, since God leads souls by many ways, but those who are unable to take this road should not be condemned or judged incapable of enjoying the great blessings contained in the mysteries of Jesus Christ our God.[45]

I do not say this without reason, for, as I have said, it is very important for us to realize that God does not lead us all by the same road, and perhaps she who believes herself to be going along the lowest road is the highest in the Lord's eyes. So it does not follow that, because all of us in this house practice prayer, we are all *perforce* to be contemplatives.[46]

43. Romano Guardini, *The Life of Faith*, trans. John Chapin (Westminster, Md.: Newman Press, 1961), p. 106.

44. Col. 3:12–17; Lk. 4:42–44.

45. *The Complete Works of St. Theresa of Jesus*, 2:307–308.

46. *Ibid.*, p. 69.

God leads each one along different paths so that hardly one spirit will be found like another in even half its method of procedure.[47]

Uniqueness of personality structure helps to specify what form and style of prayer are most appropriate for the individual. God works with and through our individuality. How dangerous, therefore, to simply adopt someone else's manner of praying. Sheer imitation is not only foolish but can be injurious to one's spiritual life, leading to frustration and discouragement. A popular expression states: "Different strokes for different folks!" So in the spiritual life: different prayers for different cares. Prayer is as varied as people, with the commonality coming in the word-response pattern underlying all communication between God and his people.

Just as prayer varies from person to person, it also varies within each person's life. During certain periods of faith development, vocal and formal prayer may well be the best form of prayer for that time; at other stages, meditative or contemplative prayer may be in order. Further, prayer styles may change within the course of a single week, even in the course of a single hour. Form and style are not the heart of the matter; what is of essence is personal encounter with God. Once that experience happens, we simply rest in his presence. "As soon as God's word makes its impact, we must leave all the rest and follow it."[48] Prayer is a means to an end, and the end is union with God. The paths to union are multiple.

Pluralism is threatened by stereotyping and rigid conformity. Granting the validity, indeed the necessity, of a certain measure of uniformity in public prayer, the principle to be followed in personal, private prayer is that of freedom. Only the individual knows the context of his or her own life; it is this context that sets the parameters for the form and style of prayer. Because our context is continually changing, prayer forms must be adapted accordingly. Thus pluralism becomes a principle necessary for spiritual health and growth.

10. Prayer leads to intimacy with God and to solidarity with all creation.[49]

It should be noted that until the soul reaches this state of union

47. *The Collected Works of St. John of the Cross*, p. 633.
48. Hans Urs von Balthasar, *Prayer*, trans. A. V. Littledale (New York: Sheed & Ward, 1961), p. 108.
49. Ps. 139; Jer. 31:31-34.

of love, she should practice love in both the active and contemplative life. Yet once she arrives, she should not become in-
volved in other works and exterior exercises that might be of the
slightest hindrance to the attentiveness of love toward God,
even though the work be of great service to God. For a little of
this pure love is more precious to God and the soul and more
beneficial to the Church, even though it seems one is doing
nothing, than all these other works put together.[50]

In prayer I can enter into contact with the God who created me
and all things out of love. In prayer I can find a new sense of
belonging since it is there that I am most related.[51]

We are put on earth a little space,
That we may learn to bear the beams of love.[52]

Activities find their meaning in terms of their goal. The end of the
spiritual life is union with God, and by means of this unity we are
mysteriously united to all creation. Oneness is attained by love;
prayer is a central love-act in our lives. Through ongoing communication with God, we grow in mutual knowledge and respect until one
day we awake to an intimacy incapable of description. The bonding
here is subtle and mysterious, powerful and challenging. The Lord
stands at the door knocking, and a choice has to be made. Following
our "Fiat," God comes to dwell with us, and our homes are never the
same.

Prayer's unifying power does not terminate in intimacy with God
alone. Authentic prayer necessitates an ever deeper union with our
brothers and sisters. To be united to the Father means to be united to
his children, the entire family of God. The closer we are to the cross of
Christ and the power of the Spirit, the closer we are to all of life. By
touching the fountain of life and holiness, we touch all creation. Thus,
without prayer a sense of alienation and isolation invades our hearts.
Separated from the source, we cannot come into vital contact with the
created world. Prayer gives us entrance not only into the heart of our
triune God but also into the mystery of his loving creation.

Because prayer fosters intimacy, it is not uncommon for fear to
block our communication with God. Intimacy means to know and to

50. *The Collected Works of St. John of the Cross*, p. 523.
51. Henri J. M. Nouwen, *The Genesee Diary: Report from a Trappist Monastery*
(New York: Doubleday & Co., 1976), p. 51.
52. William Blake, "The Little Black Boy."

be known whole; such radical sharing implies the possibility of radical rejection. Perhaps we are not sure that we are all that lovable. Thus it is in faith and trust that we approach our God, believing that he loves us unconditionally; it is with humility and courage that we approach our brothers and sisters, knowing that through grace we can accept them and that they can accept us. Prayer involves revelation, acceptance, and humility; it demands faith, trust, and courage. Gifted by the Spirit, we enter the land of prayer and therein find our happiness.

THE JOURNEY AND THE MAP

In discussing any one aspect of the spiritual life, we must view it contextually. We have pointed out ten signs on the road to union: prayer as loving attention, prayer's relationship to love, prayer's need for discipline, prayer and proper identity, prayer's focus, the conditions for prayer, prayer's tonality, source of prayer, the principle of pluralism, and prayer's goal. A corresponding set of principles marking out other aspects of the terrain in the spiritual life could easily be worked out, and these would provide meaning in such areas as ministry and asceticism. The map is large; we have considered but one aspect. Regardless of the principle and its specification, the destination is always the same: the experience of Love. That experience comes alive when we move from the map to the land it describes.

Day of Joy in the Mystery of Creation
"Lord, who has form'd me out of mud"

FIRST HOUR

Theme: Calling on God — PRAYER (vocative — "Lord").
Desire: To pray from the heart.

INTRODUCTION

In silence, enter into the Lord's presence. Realize what you are about — to be with the Lord. Ask for the gift of the Spirit, the Spirit of faith and worship. Then gently pray this psalm with the whole Church: "Let the hearts that seek Yahweh rejoice!"

Give thanks to Yahweh, call his name aloud,
proclaim his deeds to the peoples!
Sing to him, play to him,
tell over all his marvels!
Glory in his holy name,
let the hearts that seek Yahweh rejoice!

Seek Yahweh and his strength,
seek his face untiringly;
remember the marvels he has done,
his wonders, the judgments from his mouth (Ps. 105:1–5).

Points

Quietly be with Jesus as he addresses the Father. Before the foundation of the world — what mystery here! Even before we were formed out of mud, Jesus and the Father were loving us. Sense and taste their love; they created out of love, out of their Spirit. In prayer we come to know who our God is and what love he has for us.

Father,
I want those you have given me
to be with me where I am,
so that they may always see the glory
you have given me
because you loved me
before the foundation of the world.
Father, Righteous One,
the world has not known you,
but I have known you,
and these have known
that you sent me.
I have made your name known to them
and will continue to make it known,
so that the love with which you loved me may be in them,
and so that I may be in them (Jn. 17:24–26).

What makes it possible for us to call God our Father and Jesus our Lord? Paul shares the power that makes prayer possible. Note, too, the call to share in the sufferings of Christ if we want to share in his Lordship, his glory.

Everyone moved by the Spirit is a son of God. The spirit you received is not the spirit of slaves bringing fear into your lives again; it is the spirit of sons, and it makes us cry out, "Abba, Father!" The Spirit himself and our spirit bear united witness that we are children of God. And if we are children we are heirs as well: heirs of God and coheirs with Christ, sharing his sufferings so as to share his glory (Rom. 8:14–17).

Worship

In the Creed we profess that Jesus is Lord; we must taste these words in our hearts.

We believe in one Lord, Jesus Christ,
the only Son of God,

eternally begotten of the Father,
God from God, Light from Light,
true God from true God,
begotten, not made, one in Being with the Father.

Conclusion

In prayer, we call upon the Lord at all times.

I, for myself, appeal to God
and Yahweh saves me;
evening, morning, noon,
I complain, I groan;
he will hear me calling (Ps. 55:16–17).

SECOND HOUR

Theme: God's ongoing creation.
Desire: To sense our being *formed* now!

Introduction

How close God is to us now! We come now in prayer to be formed and shaped more profoundly into his image and likeness.

Yahweh, you examine me and know me,
you know if I am standing or sitting,
you read my thoughts from far away,
whether I walk or lie down, you are watching,
you know every detail of my conduct.
The word is not even on my tongue,
Yahweh, before you know all about it;
close behind and close in front you fence me round,
shielding me with your hand.
Such knowledge is beyond my understanding,
a height to which my mind cannot attain (Ps. 139:1–6).

Jesus firmly yet gently shapes the lives of Mary and Martha. What does he wish to say to me here—contemplation and/or action . . . balance?

In the course of their journey he came to a village, and a woman named Martha welcomed him into her house. She had a sister called Mary, who sat down at the Lord's feet and listened to him speaking. Now Martha who was distracted with all the serving said, "Lord, do you not care that my sister is leaving me to do the serving all by myself? Please tell her to help me." But the Lord answered: "Martha, Martha," he said, "you worry and fret about so many things, and yet few are needed, indeed only one. It is Mary who has chosen the better part; it is not to be taken from her" (Lk. 10:38–42).

God formed the prophets of old. Now he forms us, too. The process is basically the same.

> Islands, listen to me,
> pay attention, remotest peoples.
> Yahweh called me before I was born,
> from my mother's womb he pronounced my name.
>
> He made my mouth a sharp sword,
> and hid me in the shadow of his hand.
> He made me into a sharpened arrow,
> and concealed me in his quiver.
>
> He said to me, "You are my servant (Israel)
> in whom I shall be glorified";
> while I was thinking, "I have toiled in vain,
> I have exhausted myself for nothing";
>
> and all the while my cause was with Yahweh,
> and my reward with my God.
> I was honored in the eyes of Yahweh,
> my God was my strength.
>
> And now Yahweh has spoken,
> he who formed me in the womb to be his servant,
> to bring Jacob back to him,
> to gather Israel to him:
>
> "It is not enough for you to be my servant,
> to restore the tribes of Jacob
> and bring back the survivors of Israel;
> I will make you the light of the nations
> so that my salvation may reach to the ends of the earth"
> (Is. 49:1–6).

WORSHIP

Lord God, maker of heaven and earth and of all created things, you make your just ones holy and you justify sinners who confess your name. Hear us as we humbly pray to you: give us eternal joy with your saints (Daytime Prayer, Sunday, Week II).

CONCLUSION

Join the entire Church in praying the Our Father.

THIRD HOUR

Theme: Humanness.
Desire: To radically accept our "muddy" condition.

INTRODUCTION

Prayer is essentially listening and responding. We listen with reverence to God's word, then respond in praise and gratitude. Dwell on the mystery of creation: "God fashioned man of dust from the soil."

At the time when Yahweh God made earth and heaven there was as yet no wild bush on the earth nor had any wild plant yet sprung up, for Yahweh God had not sent rain on the earth, nor was there any man to till the soil. However, a flood was rising from the earth and watering all the surface of the soil. Yahweh God fashioned man of dust from the soil. Then he breathed into his nostrils a breath of life, and thus man became a living being (Gen. 2:5-7).

POINTS

In awe and wonder, contemplate how Jesus takes on our muddy condition. Our God becomes man. What dignity we have in Jesus! In prayer we revere our humanness; through it we come to divine life.

In the sixth month the angel Gabriel was sent by God to a town in Galilee called Nazareth, to a virgin betrothed to a man named

Joseph, of the House of David; and the virgin's name was Mary. He went in and said to her, "Rejoice, so highly favored! The Lord is with you."

She was deeply disturbed by these words and asked herself what this greeting could mean, but the angel said to her, "Mary, do not be afraid; you have won God's favor. Listen! You are to conceive and bear a son, and you must name him Jesus. He will be great and will be called Son of the Most High. The Lord God will give him the throne of his ancestor David; he will rule over the House of Jacob for ever and his reign will have no end."

Mary said to the angel, "But how can this come about, since I am a virgin?"

"The Most High will cover you with its shadow. And so the child will be holy and will be called Son of God. Know this too: your kinswoman Elizabeth has, in her old age, herself conceived a son, and she whom people called barren is now in her sixth month, *for nothing is impossible to God.*"

"I am the handmaid of the Lord," said Mary, "let what you have said be done to me." And the angel left her (Lk. 1:26–38).

An ancient hymn of the Church reveals the mystery of Jesus' assuming the human condition. Emptiness, incompleteness, weakness, inadequacies, fatigue, monotony — Jesus knew them all from the inside.

His state was divine,
yet he did not cling
to his equality with God
but emptied himself
to assume the condition of a slave,
and became as men are;
and being as all men are,
he was humbler yet,
even to accepting death,
death on a cross.
But God raised him high
and gave him the name
which is above all other names
so that *all beings*
in the heavens, on earth and in the underworld,
should bend the knee at the name of Jesus
and that every tongue should acclaim
Jesus Christ as Lord,
to the glory of God the Father (Phil. 2:6–11).

Worship
Saint Leo the Great reflects on the mystery of mysteries. Enter behind his words to the reality:

> In the fullness of time, chosen in the unfathomable depths of God's wisdom, the Son of God took for himself our common humanity in order to reconcile it with its creator (Office of Readings, Christmas).

Conclusion
Jesus comes from a stump and roots — such humanness.

> A shoot springs from the stock of Jesse,
> a scion thrusts from his roots (Is. 11:1).

FOURTH HOUR

Theme: Humility.
Desire: To live in the truth of our creatureliness.

Introduction
In prayer we call upon the Lord. Sense his presence and his love. In his goodness and mercy he hears us and responds to our every need. Ask for the Spirit of faith and worship.

> God, guardian of my rights, you answer when I call,
> when I am in trouble, you come to my relief;
> now be good to me and hear my prayer (Ps. 4:1).

Points
Jesus continues the work of the Father's creation through healing. One man lived in the truth; he recognized and responded to the source of life. What is the quality of my humility, the extent of my pride?

> Now on the way to Jerusalem he traveled along the border between Samaria and Galilee. As he entered one of the villages, ten lepers came to meet him. They stood some way off and called to him, "Jesus! Master! Take pity on us." When he saw them he said, "Go and show yourselves to the priests." Now as they were going

away they were cleansed. Finding himself cured, one of them turned back praising God at the top of his voice and threw himself at the feet of Jesus and thanked him. The man was a Samaritan. This made Jesus say, "Were not all ten made clean? The other nine, where are they? It seems that no one has come back to give praise to God, except this foreigner." And he said to the man, "Stand up and go on your way. Your faith has saved you" (Lk. 17:11-19).

Paul humbly and boldly tells of how God formed and shaped his life. His steppingstones reveal God's deep love and Paul's profound response. This God works in our life today. Surrender to his love and power.

"My brothers, my fathers, listen to what I have to say to you in my defense." When they realized he was speaking in Hebrew, the silence was even greater than before. "I am a Jew," Paul said, "and was born at Tarsus in Cilicia. I was brought up here in this city. I studied under Gamaliel and was taught the exact observance of the Law of our ancestors. In fact, I was as full of duty towards God as you are today. I even persecuted this Way to the death, and sent women as well as men to prison in chains as the high priest and the whole council of elders can testify, since they even sent me letters to their brothers in Damascus. When I set off it was with the intention of bringing prisoners back from there to Jerusalem for punishment.

"I was on that journey and nearly at Damascus when about midday a bright light from heaven suddenly shone round me. I fell to the ground and heard a voice saying, 'Saul, Saul, why are you persecuting me?' I answered: Who are you, Lord? and he said to me, 'I am Jesus the Nazarene, and you are persecuting me.' The people with me saw the light but did not hear his voice as he spoke to me. I said: What am I to do, Lord? The Lord answered, 'Stand up and go into Damascus, and there you will be told what you have been appointed to do.' The light had been so dazzling that I was blind and my companions had to take me by the hand; and so I came to Damascus" (Acts 22:1-11).

WORSHIP
We pray with the Church:

Come forth and see all the great works that God has brought forth by his might; fall on your knees before his glorious throne: Alleluia! (Morning Prayer, Epiphany).

Conclusion
A deep and humble hymn.

> Sincere, my call — Yahweh, answer me!
>   I will respect your statutes.
> I invoke you, save me,
>   I will observe your decrees.
> I am up before dawn to call for help,
>   I put my hope in your word.
> I lie awake throughout the night,
>   to meditate on your promise.
> In your love, Yahweh, listen to my voice,
>   let your rulings give me life.
> My cruel persecutors are closing in,
>   how remote they are from your Law!
> But, Yahweh, you are closer still
>   and all your commandments are true.
> Long have I known that your decrees
>   were founded to last for ever.
>
> Take note of my suffering and rescue me,
>   for I do not forget your Law.
> Take up my cause, defend me,
>   give me life as you have promised (Ps. 119:145–152).

Day of Gratitude for the Mystery of Redemption

"And has redeem'd me through thy blood"

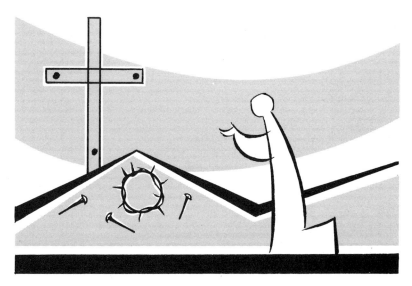

FIRST HOUR

Theme: Jesus our Savior.
Desire: To know that our Redeemer lives.

INTRODUCTION

Prayer is a time of intimacy, of deep mutual sharing. The Lord is here now, desirous to share in our lives and for us to share in his life. Love is evidenced in dying for another; Jesus shed his blood that we might live.

> The blessing-cup that we bless is a communion with the blood of Christ, and the bread that we break is a communion with the body of Christ (1 Cor. 10:16).

POINTS

The example! Jesus' redeeming power is already operative before the Cross: a constant dying to self that others might live. Our call is to follow in service.

37

It was before the festival of the Passover, and Jesus knew that the hour had come for him to pass from this world to the Father. He had always loved those who were his in the world, but now he showed how perfect his love was.

They were at supper, and the devil had already put it into the mind of Judas Iscariot, son of Simon, to betray him. Jesus knew that the Father had put everything into his hands, and that he had come from God and was returning to God, and he got up from table, removed his outer garment and, taking a towel, wrapped it round his waist; he then poured water into a basin and began to wash the disciples' feet and to wipe them with the towel he was wearing.

He came to Simon Peter, who said to him, "Lord, are you going to wash my feet?"

Jesus answered, "At the moment you do not know what I am doing, but later you will understand."

"Never!" said Peter. "You shall never wash my feet."

Jesus replied, "If I do not wash you, you can have nothing in common with me."

"Then, Lord," said Simon Peter, "not only my feet, but my hands and my head as well!"

Jesus said, "No one who has taken a bath needs washing, he is clean all over. You too are clean, though not all of you are." He knew who was going to betray him, that was why he said, "though not all of you are."

When he had washed their feet and put on his clothes again he went back to the table. "Do you understand," he said, "what I have done to you? You call me Master and Lord, and rightly; so I am. If I, then, the Lord and Master, have washed your feet, you should wash each other's feet. I have given you an example so that you may copy what I have done to you" (Jn. 13:1–15).

Jesus saves us through the covenant of his blood. Pray to experience this mystery in faith. Jesus continues to save us daily in the Eucharist and in the Church.

For this is what I received from the Lord, and in turn passed on to you: that on the same night that he was betrayed, the Lord Jesus took some bread, and thanked God for it and broke it, and he said, "This is my body, which is for you; do this as a memorial of me." In the same way he took the cup after supper, and said, "This cup is the new covenant in my blood. Whenever you drink it, do this as a memorial of me." Until the Lord comes, therefore, every time you eat this bread and drink this cup, you are proclaiming his death, and so anyone who eats the bread or drinks the cup of the Lord unworthily will be behaving unworthily towards the body and blood of the Lord (1 Cor. 11:23–27).

WORSHIP
Join the Church in prayer:

Let Israel rejoice in you, Lord, and acknowledge you as creator and redeemer. We put our trust in your faithfulness and proclaim the wonderful truths of salvation. May your loving kindness embrace us now and for ever (Daytime Prayer, Sunday, Week II).

CONCLUSION
How can we thank our Redeemer sufficiently?

What return can I make to Yahweh
  for all his goodness to me?
I will offer libations to my savior,
invoking the name of Yahweh (Ps. 116:12–13).

SECOND HOUR

Theme: The Cross.
Desire: To experience Christ crucified.

INTRODUCTION
Loving attention is at the heart of prayer. Ask for the Spirit of love and for the gift of attentiveness. Sense the agony in the psalmist's heart: broken, insulted, with no sympathy or comforters.

You know all the insults I endure,
every one of my oppressors is known to you;
the insults have broken my heart,
my shame and disgrace are past cure;
I had hoped for sympathy, but in vain,
I found no one to console me (Ps. 69:19–20).

Points

In deep compassion, join Mary and John. What do they see, what do they hear, what goes on in their hearts? Look upon the Lord and share his pain; the Cross is still very much a part of the world.

> Near the cross of Jesus stood his mother and his mother's sister, Mary the wife of Clopas, and Mary of Magdala. Seeing his mother and the disciple he loved standing near her, Jesus said to his mother, "Woman, this is your son." Then to the disciple he said, "This is your mother." And from that moment the disciple made a place for her in his home (Jn. 19:25–27).

Christ is our Priest. He understands us from the inside. Through his sufferings we have been saved; we also learn obedience through suffering with Christ.

> Since in Jesus, the Son of God, we have the supreme high priest who has gone through to the highest heaven, we must never let go of the faith that we have professed. For it is not as if we had a high priest who was incapable of feeling our weaknesses with us; but we have one who has been tempted in every way that we are, though he is without sin. Let us be confident, then, in approaching the throne of grace, that we shall have mercy from him and find grace when we are in need of help . . . . During his life on earth, he offered up prayer and entreaty, aloud and in silent tears, to the one who had the power to save him out of death, and he submitted so humbly that his prayer was heard. Although he was Son, he learned to obey through suffering; but having been made perfect, he became for all who obey him the source of eternal salvation and was acclaimed by God with the title of high priest of the order of Melchizedek (Heb. 4:14–16; 5:7–9).

Worship

Ponder this prayer of Holy Week:

> Father,
> in your plan of salvation
> your Son Jesus Christ accepted the cross
> and freed us from the power of the enemy.
> May we come to share the glory of his resurrection,
> for he lives and reigns with you and the Holy Spirit,
> one God, for ever and ever (Wednesday of Holy Week).

CONCLUSION
The depth of Jesus' love!

> I give you a new commandment: love one another as I have loved
> you (Jn. 13:34).

THIRD HOUR

Theme: Sin.
Desire: To know the cause of the Cross.

INTRODUCTION
We come to prayer open and naked. In faith we know that God is a
God of love and mercy. So we pray with hope and confidence. We
listen in trust and awe.

> At last I admitted to you I had sinned;
>   no longer concealing my guilt,
> I said, "I will go to Yahweh
>   and confess my fault."
> And you, you have forgiven the wrong I did,
>   have pardoned my sin (Ps. 32:5).

POINTS
Why the Cross? Betrayal, dishonesty, thirty pieces of what? We
look into our own hearts and there discover the cause of the Cross. Sin
is our refusal to be faithful and loving.

> Then one of the Twelve, the man called Judas Iscariot, went to
> the chief priests and said, "What are you prepared to give me if I
> hand him over to you?" They paid him thirty silver pieces, and
> from that moment he looked for an opportunity to betray him.
>   Now on the first day of Unleavened Bread the disciples came to
> Jesus to say, "Where do you want us to make the preparations for
> you to eat the passover?"

"Go to so-and-so in the city," he replied, "and say to him, 'The Master says: My time is near. It is at your house that I am keeping Passover with my disciples.'" The disciples did what Jesus told them and prepared the Passover.

When evening came he was at table with the twelve disciples. And while they were eating he said, "I tell you solemnly, one of you is about to betray me."

They were greatly distressed and started asking him in turn, "Not I, Lord, surely?"

He answered, "Someone who has dipped his hand into the dish with me, will betray me. The Son of Man is going to his fate, as the scriptures say he will, but alas for that man by whom the Son of Man is betrayed! Better for that man if he had never been born!"

Judas, who was to betray him, asked in his turn, "Not I, Rabbi, surely?"

"They are your own words," answered Jesus (Mt. 26:14–25).

All of history testifies to sin. Times have not changed that radically. The human heart remains essentially the same. What seeds of sin still remain to be rooted out?

Sons of Israel, listen to the word of Yahweh,
for Yahweh indicts the inhabitants of the country:
there is no fidelity, no tenderness,
no knowledge of God in the country,
only perjury and lies, slaughter, theft,
adultery and violence, murder after murder.
This is why the country is in mourning,
and all who live in it pine away,
even the wild animals and the birds of heaven;
the fish of the sea themselves are perishing (Hos. 4:1–3).

Worship

The Church prays:

God of mercy,
you wash away our sins in water,
you give us new birth in the Spirit,
and redeem us in the blood of Christ.
As we celebrate Christ's resurrection
increase our awareness of these blessings,
and renew your gift of life within us.
(Office of Readings, Sunday within the Octave of Easter)

CONCLUSION
How does God deal with our sins? Listen and praise him!

> It is you who have kept my soul
> from the pit of nothingness,
> you have thrust all my sins
> behind your back (Is. 38:17).

FOURTH HOUR

Theme: Gratitude.
Desire: To give thanks for what Jesus has done for us.

INTRODUCTION
Prayer deals more with the Giver than with the gift. We focus on God and lovingly dwell in his presence, open to his every desire. Listen and your soul will live.

> Give thanks to Yahweh, for he is good,
> his love is everlasting!
> Let the House of Israel say it,
> "His love is everlasting!" (Ps. 118:1).

POINTS
Our God is a God of compassion. Enter the experience and see everything from the inside. What went on in the woman's heart? What gratitude and rejoicing! What deep faith and love!

> Then he turned to the woman. "Simon," he said, "you see this woman? I came into your house, and you poured no water over my feet, but she has poured out her tears over my feet and wiped them away with her hair. You gave me no kiss, but she has been covering my feet with kisses ever since I came in. You did not anoint my head with oil, but she has anointed my feet with ointment. For this reason I tell you that her sins, her many sins, must have been forgiven her, or she would not have shown such great love. It is the man who is forgiven little who shows little love." Then he said to her, "Your sins are forgiven." Those who were with him at table began to say to themselves, "Who is this man,

that he even forgives sins?" But he said to the woman, "Your faith has saved you; go in peace" (Lk. 7:44–50).

Our memory must be clear. Remember the ransom paid for us, the price of our salvation! Gratitude is central to the Christian way of life — gratitude in word and deed.

If you are acknowledging as your Father one who has no favorites and judges everyone according to what he has done, you must be scrupulously careful as long as you are living away from your home. Remember, the ransom that was paid to free you from the useless way of life your ancestors handed down was not paid in anything corruptible, neither in silver nor gold, but in the precious blood of a lamb without spot or stain, namely Christ; who, though known since before the world was made, has been revealed only in our time, the end of the ages, for your sake. Through him you now have faith in God, who raised him from the dead and gave him glory for that very reason — so that you would have faith and hope in God (1 Pet. 1:17–21).

WORSHIP
With the Church we pray:

God of mercy and goodness, when Christ called out to you in torment, you heard him and gave him victory over death because of his love for you. We already know the affection you have for us; fill us with a greater love of your name and we will proclaim you more boldly before men and happily lead them to celebrate your glory (Morning Prayer, Wednesday, Week III).

CONCLUSION
All creatures praise and thank our God.

May you be blessed, Lord, God of our ancestors,
be praised and extolled for ever.
Blessed be your glorious and holy name,
praised and extolled for ever.
May you be blessed in the Temple of your sacred glory,
exalted and glorified above all else for ever:
blessed on the throne of your kingdom,
praised and exalted above all else for ever.
All things the Lord has made, bless the Lord:
give glory and eternal praise to him (Dan. 3:52–54, 57).

Day of Commitment to the Mystery of Holiness

"And sanctifi'd me to do good"

FIRST HOUR

Theme: Call to holiness.
Desire: To sense the meaning of divine indwelling.

INTRODUCTION

Prayer is a seeking and a being found. Ask for the Spirit of love. What is it that we really desire in life? Prayer is to dwell in the house of the Lord — in this is the source of holiness.

> One thing I ask of Yahweh,
>   one thing I seek:
> to live in the house of Yahweh
>   all the days of my life,
> to enjoy the sweetness of Yahweh
>   and to consult him in his Temple (Ps. 27:4).

Points

Holiness is a being with. Enter into the heart of Jesus and his longing for the Father and his longing for us. Great mystery here! Stand in awe.

Do not let your hearts be troubled.
Trust in God still, and trust in me.
There are many rooms in my Father's house;
if there were not, I should have told you.
I am going now to prepare a place for you,
and after I have gone and prepared you a place,
I shall return to take you with me;
so that where I am
you may be too . . . .

Do you not believe
that I am in the Father and the Father is in me?
The words I say to you I do not speak as from myself:
it is the Father, living in me, who is doing this work.
You must believe me when I say
that I am in the Father and the Father is in me;
believe it on the evidence of this work, if for no other reason.
I tell you most solemnly,
whoever believes in me
will perform the same works as I do myself,
he will perform even greater works,
because I am going to the Father (Jn. 14:1-3, 10-14).

Our life is life in Christ. We are called to deep personal union. If we desire to live in Christ, we must also accept death in him. A call to intimacy.

You have been taught that when we were baptized in Christ Jesus we were baptized in his death; in other words, when we were baptized we went into the tomb with him and joined him in death, so that as Christ was raised from the dead by the Father's glory, we too might live a new life.

If in union with Christ we have imitated his death, we shall also imitate him in his resurrection. We must realize that our former selves have been crucified with him to destroy this sinful body and to free us from the slavery of sin. When a man dies, of course, he has finished with sin.

But we believe that having died with Christ we shall return to live with him: Christ, as we know, having been raised from the dead will never die again. Death has no power over him any more. When he died, he died, once for all, to sin, so his life now is life with God; and in that way, you too must consider yourselves to be dead to sin but alive for God in Christ Jesus (Rom. 6:3–11).

Worship
In the liturgy we pray:

You have been enlightened by Christ.
Walk always as children of the light
and keep the flame of faith alive in your hearts.
When the Lord comes, may you go out to meet him
with all the saints in the heavenly kingdom.
(Rite of Baptism of Adults)

Conclusion
Holiness is grounded and expressed in love — Love!

My dear people,
let us love one another
since love comes from God
and everyone who loves is begotten by God and knows God
(1 Jn. 4:7).

SECOND HOUR

Theme: The Holy Spirit sanctifies us.
Desire: To be transformed by the Spirit of the Father and of the Son.

Introduction
Prayer brings about the renewing of the face of the earth. In silence and peace, let the Lord speak to your heart. His breath gives life and love. Be open.

You give breath, fresh life begins,
you keep renewing the world (Ps. 104:30).

Points

Jesus gifts the disciples and us with the gift of the Spirit. Herein is our peace and strength.

> In the evening of that same day, the first day of the week, the doors were closed in the room where the disciples were, for fear of the Jews. Jesus came and stood among them. He said to them, "Peace be with you," and showed them his hands and his side. The disciples were filled with joy when they saw the Lord, and he said to them again, "Peace be with you."
>
> "As the Father sent me,
> so am I sending you."
>
> After saying this he breathed on them and said:
>
> "Receive the Holy Spirit.
> For those whose sins you forgive,
> they are forgiven;
> for those whose sins you retain,
> they are retained" (Jn. 20:19–23).

Paul lived in the Spirit and shared that reality with others. The power of the Spirit continues to transform the world through the variety of gifts bestowed on the Church.

> There is a variety of gifts but always the same Spirit; there are all sorts of services to be done, but always to the same Lord; working in all sorts of different ways in different people, it is the same God who is working in all of them. The particular way in which the Spirit is given to each person is for a good purpose. One may have the gift of preaching with wisdom given him by the Spirit; another may have the gift of preaching instruction given him by the same Spirit; and another the gift of faith given by the same Spirit; another again the gift of healing, through this one Spirit; one, the power of miracles; another, prophecy; another the gift of recognizing spirits; another the gift of tongues and another the ability to interpret them. All these are the work of one and the same Spirit, who distributes different gifts to different people just as he chooses (1 Cor. 12:4–11).

Worship

Ponder this selection from the Sequence of Pentecost:

> Come, Holy Spirit, and from heaven direct on man the rays of

your light. Come, Father of the poor; come, giver of God's gifts; come, light of men's hearts.

CONCLUSION
Respond to this call to prayer.

> But you, my dear friends, must use your most holy faith as your foundation and build on that, praying in the Holy Spirit; keep yourselves within the love of God and wait for the mercy of our Lord Jesus Christ to give you eternal life (Jude 20–21).

THIRD HOUR

Theme: The road to virtue.
Desire: To live holy, virtuous lives.

INTRODUCTION
Prayer leads to service. In prayer we sit at table with the Lord and then are sent out to do the truth. Let us listen to the prophet call us to deep, holy lives.

> Take your wrongdoing out of my sight.
> Cease to do evil.
> Learn to do good,
> search for justice,
> help the oppressed,
> be just to the orphan,
> plead for the widow (Is. 1:16–17).

POINTS
Christianity is very concrete; it involves the nitty-gritty. Listen reverently to Jesus as he reveals the mission of his Father.

> When the Son of Man comes in his glory, escorted by all the angels, then he will take his seat on his throne of glory. All the nations will be assembled before him and he will separate men one from another as the shepherd separates sheep from goats. He will place the sheep on his right and the goats on his left. Then the King will say to those on his right hand, "Come, you whom my

Father has blessed, take for your heritage the kingdom prepared for you since the foundation of the world. For I was hungry and you gave me food; I was thirsty and you gave me drink; I was a stranger and you made me welcome; naked and you clothed me, sick and you visited me, in prison and you came to see me." Then the virtuous will say to him in reply, "When did we see you hungry and feed you; or thirsty and give you drink? When did we see you a stranger and make you welcome; naked and clothe you; sick or in prison and go to see you?" And the King will answer, "I tell you solemnly, in so far as you did this to one of the least of these brothers of mine, you did it to me" (Mt. 25:31–40).

The test of our faith and life in God is in our reaching out to others. There is a delicate balance between contemplation and action; there is a need for both.

Take the case, my brothers, of someone who has never done a single good act but claims that he has faith. Will that faith save him? If one of the brothers or one of the sisters is in need of clothes and has not enough food to live on, and one of you says to them, "I wish you well; keep yourself warm and eat plenty," without giving them these bare necessities of life, then what good is that? Faith is like that: if good works do not go with it, it is quite dead.

This is the way to talk to people of that kind: "You say you have faith and have good deeds; I will prove to you that I have faith by showing you my good deeds — now you prove to me that you have faith without any good deeds to show. You believe in the one God — that is creditable enough, but the demons have the same belief, and they tremble with fear. Do realize, you senseless man, that faith without good deeds is useless. You surely know that Abraham our father was justified by his deed, because he offered his son Isaac on the altar? There you see it: faith and deeds were working together; his faith became perfect by what he did. This is what scripture really means when it says: Abraham put his faith in God, and this was counted as making him justified; and that is why he was called "the friend of God."

You see now that it is by doing something good, and not only by believing, that a man is justified. There is another example of the same kind: Rahab the prostitute, justified by her deeds because she welcomed the messengers and showed them a different way to leave. A body dies when it is separated from the spirit, and in the same way faith is dead if it is separated from good deeds (Jas. 2:14–26).

WORSHIP
The source of virtue is in God, and so we pray:

God, we praise you:
Father all-powerful, Christ Lord and Savior,
    Spirit of love.
You reveal yourself in the depths of our being,
drawing us to share in your life and your love.
One God, three Persons,
be near to the people formed in your image,
close to the world your love brings to life.
(Opening Prayer, Trinity Sunday)

CONCLUSION
A good summary of our call to fullness of life:

. . . this is what Yahweh asks of you:
only this, to act justly,
to love tenderly
and to walk humbly with your God (Mic. 6:8).

FOURTH HOUR

Theme: Being sent (mission).
Desire: To know that we are God's agents of love and forgiveness.

INTRODUCTION
*Prayer demands silence, solitude, and surrender, which are gifts of
the Spirit. Allow the Spirit to work within your heart as the Father
now speaks in his word.*

Happy the man who cares for the poor and the weak:
if disaster strikes, Yahweh will come to his help (Ps. 41:1).

POINTS
*The good news of God's love and forgiveness. We have been sancti-
fied to do good by sharing these gifts with others in word and deed.
We are agents of grace.*

After the sabbath, and towards dawn on the first day of the week, Mary of Magdala and the other Mary went to visit the sepulcher. And all at once there was a violent earthquake, for the angel of the Lord, descending from heaven, came and rolled away the stone and sat on it. His face was like lightning, his robe white as snow. The guards were so shaken, so frightened of him, that they were like dead men. But the angel spoke; and he said to the women, "There is no need for you to be afraid. I know you are looking for Jesus, who was crucified. He is not here, for he has risen, as he said he would. Come and see the place where he lay, then go quickly and tell his disciples, 'He has risen from the dead and now he is going before you to Galilee; it is there you will see him.' Now I have told you." Filled with awe and great joy the women came quickly away from the tomb and ran to tell the disciples.

And there, coming to meet them, was Jesus. "Greetings," he said. And the women came up to him and, falling down before him, clasped his feet. Then Jesus said to them, "Do not be afraid; go and tell my brothers that they must leave for Galilee; they will see me there" (Mt. 28:1–10).

The call to preach and bear witness — this is a privilege and a responsibility. What dignity we have and how much God looks to us for help. Deep fellowship here.

Then Peter addressed them: "You must have heard about the recent happenings in Judaea; about Jesus of Nazareth and how he began in Galilee, after John had been preaching baptism. God had anointed him with the Holy Spirit and with power, and because God was with him, Jesus went about doing good and curing all who had fallen into the power of the devil. Now I, and those with me, can witness to everything he did throughout the countryside of Judaea and in Jerusalem itself: and also to the fact that they killed him by hanging him on a tree, yet three days afterward God raised him to life and allowed him to be seen, not by the whole people but only by certain witnesses God had chosen beforehand. Now we are those witnesses — we have eaten and drunk with him after his resurrection from the dead — and he has ordered us to proclaim this to his people and to tell them that God has appointed him to judge everyone, alive and dead. It is to him that all the prophets bear this witness: that all who believe in Jesus will have their sins forgiven through his name (Acts 10:34, 37–43).

Worship

With the Church we pray:

> Lord,
> increase our eagerness to do your will
> and help us to know the saving power of your love.
> Grant this through our Lord Jesus Christ, your Son,
> who lives and reigns with you and the Holy Spirit,
> one God, for ever and ever. Amen.
> (Office of Readings, Wednesday, 34th Week)

Conclusion

Like Timothy, we are called to fight the good fight.

> But, as a man dedicated to God, you must avoid all that. You must aim to be saintly and religious, filled with faith and love, patient and gentle. Fight the good fight of the faith and win for yourself the eternal life to which you were called when you made your profession and spoke up for the truth in front of many witnesses (1 Tim. 6:11-12).

Day of Sorrow for Sin

"Purge all my sins done heretofore:
For I confess my heavy score,
And I will strive to sin no more."

FIRST HOUR

Theme: Purgation.
Desire: To experience life through death.

INTRODUCTION

God calls us to prayer; he always takes the initiative. His word both consoles and purges. He loves us too much not to remove any seeds of spiritual cancer. Be open to his loving, burning gaze.

The pride that you take in yourselves is hardly to your credit. You must know how even a small amount of yeast is enough to leaven all the dough, so get rid of all the old yeast, and make yourselves into a completely new batch of bread, unleavened as you are meant to be. Christ, our passover, has been sacrificed; let us celebrate the feast, then, by getting rid of all the old yeast of evil and wickedness, having only the unleavened bread of sincerity and truth (1 Cor. 5:6–8).

Points

Allow the imagery of the vine and branches to draw you into the mystery. So connected, so much life from the vine. Sense the love behind the pruning—pain allowed only for our own good.

> I am the true vine,
> and my Father is the vinedresser.
> Every branch in me that bears no fruit
> he cuts away,
> and every branch that does bear fruit he prunes
> to make it bear even more.
> You are pruned already,
> by means of the word that I have spoken to you.
> Make your home in me, as I make mine in you.
> As a branch cannot bear fruit all by itself,
> but must remain part of the vine,
> neither can you unless you remain in me.
> I am the vine,
> you are the branches.
> Whoever remains in me, with me in him,
> bears fruit in plenty;
> for cut off from me you can do nothing.
> Anyone who does not remain in me
> is like a branch that has been thrown away
> —he withers;
> these branches are collected and thrown on the fire,
> and they are burnt.
> If you remain in me
> and my words remain in you,
> you may ask what you will
> and you shall get it.
> It is to the glory of my Father that you should bear much fruit,
> and then you will be my disciples (Jn. 15:1–8).

Jesus has gone before us; he knows suffering and purgation from experience. We see in his suffering the meaning of our sin. The Old Testament prophet Isaiah foretells the cost of holiness.

See, my servant will prosper,
he shall be lifted up, exalted, rise to great heights.

As the crowds were appalled on seeing him
— so disfigured did he look
that he seemed no longer human —
so will the crowds be astonished at him,
and kings stand speechless before him;
for they shall see something never told
and witness something never heard before:
"Who could believe what we have heard,
and to whom has the power of Yahweh been revealed?"
Like a sapling he grew up in front of us,
like a root in arid ground.
Without beauty, without majesty (we saw him),
no looks to attract our eyes;
a thing despised and rejected by men,
a man of sorrows and familiar with suffering,
a man to make people screen their faces;
he was despised and we took no account of him.

And yet ours were the sufferings he bore,
ours the sorrows he carried.
But we, we thought of him as someone punished,
struck by God, and brought low.
Yet he was pierced through for our faults,
crushed for our sins.
On him lies a punishment that brings us peace,
and through his wounds we are healed (Is. 52:13–53:5).

Worship

Saint John of the Cross preached the doctrine of self-denial and purgation. With the Church we pray:

Father,
you endowed John of the Cross with a spirit of
self-denial and a love of the cross.
By following his example,
may we come to the eternal vision of your glory.
(Opening Prayer, Feast of St. John of the Cross)

Conclusion

Part of the paschal mystery is the experience of suffering.

My tent is pulled up, and thrown away
like the tent of a shepherd;
like a weaver you roll up my life
to cut it from the loom.

From dawn to night you are compassing my end,
I cry aloud until the morning;
like a lion he crushes all my bones,
from dawn to night you are compassing my end (Is. 38:12–13).

SECOND HOUR

Theme: Confession of sin.
Desire: To name and claim where we are not free.

INTRODUCTION

In prayer we come before God just as we are. Our God is gentle and merciful; we need not fear. In the truth of things we are set free.

Have mercy on me, O God, in your goodness,
in your great tenderness wipe away my faults;
wash me clean of my guilt,
purify me from my sin.

For I am well aware of my faults,
I have my sin constantly in mind,
having sinned against none other than you,
having done what you regard as wrong (Ps. 51:1–4).

POINTS

To whom does Jesus come? To our house! Enter the situation and taste his deep love. A heart full of understanding and compassion.

When Jesus was at dinner in his house, a number of tax collectors and sinners were also sitting at the table with Jesus and his disciples; for there were many of them among his followers. When the scribes of the Pharisee party saw him eating with sinners and tax collectors, they said to his disciples, "Why does he eat with tax collectors and sinners?" When Jesus heard this he said to them, "It is not the healthy who need the doctor, but the sick. I did not come to call the virtuous, but sinners" (Mk. 2:15-17).

Knowing that we have been forgiven, we must forgive others. Paul knew from experience how difficult it is to live with others, in community. What a call!

You are God's chosen race, his saints; he loves you, and you should be clothed in sincere compassion, in kindness and humility, gentleness and patience. Bear with one another; forgive each other as soon as a quarrel begins. The Lord has forgiven you; now you must do the same. Over all these clothes, to keep them together and complete them, put on love. And may the peace of Christ reign in your hearts, because it is for this that you were called together as parts of one body. Always be thankful (Col. 3:12-15).

Worship

In the rite for the sacrament of reconciliation we find this prayer:

Lord, hear the prayers of those who call on you, forgive the sins of those who confess to you, and in merciful love give us your pardon and your peace.

Conclusion

How loving and good is our merciful Lord!

You are my God, I give you thanks,
  I extol you, my God;
I give you thanks for having heard me,
  you have been my savior.
Give thanks to Yahweh, for he is good,
  his love is everlasting! (Ps. 118:28-29).

THIRD HOUR

Theme: Conversion.
Desire: To be continually redeemed by God's saving love.

INTRODUCTION

Prayer is a time of growth in the Lord. We turn from our selfishness to focus on God and his will. In prayer we are converted and gently healed. Praise God for how he worked in the heart of David, how he is working in our own heart.

But afterward David's heart misgave him for having taken a census of the people. "I have committed a grave sin," David said to Yahweh. "But now, Yahweh, I beg you to forgive your servant for this fault. I have been very foolish" (2 Sam. 24:10–11).

POINTS

The prophet is sent by God to call people to the truth. Conversion is a root reality. Only through the Spirit can we truly turn to God.

In due course John the Baptist appeared; he preached in the wilderness of Judaea and this was his message: "Repent, for the kingdom of heaven is close at hand." This was the man the prophet Isaiah spoke of when he said:

> A voice cries in the wilderness:
> Prepare a way for the Lord,
> make his paths straight.

This man John wore a garment made of camel-hair with a leather belt round his waist, and his food was locusts and wild honey. Then Jerusalem and all Judaea and the whole Jordan district made their way to him, and as they were baptized by him in the river Jordan they confessed their sins. But when he saw a number of Pharisees and Sadducees coming for baptism he said to them, "Brood of vipers, who warned you to fly from the retribution that is coming? But if you are repentant, produce the appropriate fruit, and do not presume to tell yourselves, 'We have Abraham for our father,' because, I tell you, God can raise children for Abraham from these stones. Even now the axe is laid to the roots of the trees, so that any tree which fails to produce good fruit will be cut down and thrown on the fire. I baptize you in water for repentance, but the one who follows me is more powerful than I am, and I am not fit to carry his sandals; he will baptize you with the Holy Spirit and fire. His winnowing-fan is in his hand; he will clear his threshing-floor and gather his wheat into the barn; but the chaff he will burn in a fire that will never go out" (Mt. 3:1–12).

God calls when and where he wills. Though a dramatic conversion is presented here, Paul's entire life was one of ongoing conversion.

Suddenly, while he was traveling to Damascus and just before he reached the city, there came a light from heaven all round him. He fell to the ground, and then he heard a voice saying, "Saul, Saul, why are you persecuting me?"

"Who are you, Lord?" he asked, and the voice answered, "I am Jesus, and you are persecuting me. Get up now and go into the city, and you will be told what you have to do." The men traveling with Saul stood there speechless, for though they heard the voice they could see no one. Saul got up from the ground, but even with his eyes wide open he could see nothing at all, and they had to lead him into Damascus by the hand. For three days he was without his sight, and took neither food nor drink (Acts 9:3–9).

Worship

We pray with all the people of God:

May the Passion of our Lord Jesus Christ,
the intercession of the Blessed Virgin Mary
   and of all the saints,
whatever good you do and suffering you endure,
heal your sins,
help you to grow in holiness,
and reward you with eternal life.
(Rite for Reconciliation)

Conclusion

Gratitude for the grace and joy of reconciliation.

When we were reconciled to God by the death of his Son, we were still enemies; now that we have been reconciled, surely we may count on being saved by the life of his Son? Not merely because we have been reconciled but because we are filled with joyful trust in God, through our Lord Jesus Christ, through whom we have already gained our reconciliation (Rom. 5:10–11).

FOURTH HOUR

Theme: Fortitude.
Desire: To be willing to struggle and die in doing the Father's will.

INTRODUCTION

Saint Teresa of Avila says that it takes much courage to go to prayer. We ask for the Spirit of fortitude to allow us to be ready to die to self in bringing about truth and goodness. With Jesus and in him, we strive to do the Father's will whatever the price.

Steadfast in heart he overcomes his fears:
in the end he will triumph over his enemies (Ps. 112:8).

POINTS

The courage of Zacchaeus to change his life. What did people think? How was he able to face the falsity in his own heart? Much fortitude here! The Spirit!

He entered Jericho and was going through the town when a man whose name was Zacchaeus made his appearance; he was one of the senior tax collectors and a wealthy man. He was anxious to see what kind of man Jesus was, but he was too short and could not see him for the crowd; so he ran ahead and climbed a sycamore tree to catch a glimpse of Jesus who was to pass that way. When Jesus reached the spot he looked up and spoke to him: "Zacchaeus, come down. Hurry, because I must stay at your house today." And he hurried down and welcomed him joyfully. They all complained when they saw what was happening. "He has gone to stay at a sinner's house," they said. But Zacchaeus stood his ground and said to the Lord, "Look, sir, I am going to give half my property to the poor, and if I have cheated anybody I will pay him back four times the amount." And Jesus said to him, "Today salvation has come to this house, because this man too is a son of Abraham; for the Son of Man has come to seek out and save what was lost" (Lk. 19:1-10).

What a powerful witness we have in Stephen, the first martyr. And then there was Thomas More and so many others. We too must beg for the gift of courage.

But Stephen, filled with the Holy Spirit, gazed into heaven and saw the glory of God, and Jesus standing at God's right hand. "I

61

can see heaven thrown open," he said, "and the Son of Man standing at the right hand of God." At this all the members of the council shouted out and stopped their ears with their hands; then they
all rushed at him, sent him out of the city and stoned him. The
witnesses put down their clothes at the feet of a young man called
Saul. As they were stoning him, Stephen said in invocation,
"Lord Jesus, receive my spirit." Then he knelt down and said
aloud, "Lord, do not hold this sin against them"; and with these
words he fell asleep. Saul entirely approved of the killing (Acts
7:55–60).

WORSHIP

The liturgy recognizes the source of all courage and strength:

All-powerful, ever-living God,
turn our weakness into strength.
As you gave your martyrs
the courage to suffer death for Christ,
give us the courage to live in faithful witness to you.
(Common of Martyrs)

CONCLUSION

The Lord preserves us in our sufferings.

Hardships in plenty beset the virtuous man,
but Yahweh rescues him from them all;
taking care of every bone,
Yahweh will not let one be broken (Ps. 34:19–20).

Day of Growth in the Lord

"Enrich my heart, mouth, hands in me"

FIRST HOUR

Theme: Growth.
Desire: To allow God's grace to enrich our lives.

INTRODUCTION
Listening is at the heart of prayer—listening with love. Then we respond and show our love in word and with our lives. What God does in prayer is more important than our words, our thoughts, our responses.

> I give thanks to your name for your love and faithfulness;
> your promise is even greater than your fame.
> The day I called for help, you heard me
> and you increased my strength (Ps. 138:2–3).

POINTS
The Lord comes to nourish us with himself. As a God of life, he

63

spends himself that we might share in the fullness of his love and peace. We grow in doing the Father's will.

> I am the bread of life.
> He who comes to me will never be hungry;
> he who believes in me will never thirst.
> But, as I have told you,
> you can see me and still you do not believe.
> All that the Father gives me will come to me,
> and whoever comes to me
> I shall not turn him away;
> because I have come from heaven,
> not to do my own will,
> but to do the will of the one who sent me.
> Now the will of him who sent me
> is that I should lose nothing
> of all that he has given to me,
> and that I should raise it up on the last day.
> Yes, it is my Father's will
> that whoever sees the Son and believes in him
> shall have eternal life,
> and that I shall raise him up on the last day (Jn. 6:35–40).

Our growth comes from the indwelling of Jesus in our hearts. In a special way we grow through suffering when experienced in union with Christ.

> Simply reverence the Lord Christ in your hearts, and always have your answer ready for people who ask you the reason for the hope that you all have. But give it with courtesy and respect and with a clear conscience, so that those who slander you when you are living a good life in Christ may be proved wrong in the accusations that they bring. And if it is the will of God that you should suffer, it is better to suffer for doing right than for doing wrong (1 Pet. 3:15–18).

WORSHIP

God continues to gift us with life and so we pray:

> Lord Jesus Christ, shepherd of your Church, you give us new birth in the waters of baptism, anoint us with saving oil, and call us to salvation at your table. Dispel the terrors of death and the darkness of error. Lead your people along safe paths, that they

may rest securely in you and live for ever in your Father's house
(Daytime Prayer, Sunday, Week II).

CONCLUSION
It is here that we are nourished and nurtured.

> Oh, come to the water all you who are thirsty;
> though you have no money, come!
> Buy corn without money, and eat,
> and, at no cost, wine and milk.
> Why spend money on what is not bread,
> your wages on what fails to satisfy?
> Listen, listen to me, and you will have good things to eat
> and rich food to enjoy.
> Pay attention, come to me;
> listen, and your soul will live.

> With you I will make an everlasting covenant
> out of the favors promised to David.
> See, I have made of you a witness to the peoples,
> a leader and a master of the nations (Is. 55:1–4).

SECOND HOUR

Theme: The heart of Christ.
Desire: To allow our hearts to be touched.

INTRODUCTION
*As the potter works on the clay, so too does the Lord work on our
hearts. Holiness is union of hearts, a oneness of affectivity. This happens in prayer.*

> God create a clean heart in me,
> put into me a new and constant spirit,
> do not banish me from your presence,
> do not deprive me of your holy spirit (Ps. 51:10–11).

Points

Jesus is concerned about where we set our hearts. What are the idols of our lives? Are our hearts filled with junk or open to the Lord's coming at any time?

So do not worry; do not say, "What are we to eat? What are we to drink? How are we to be clothed?" It is the pagans who set their hearts on all these things. Your heavenly Father knows you need them all. Set your hearts on his kingdom first, and on his righteousness, and all these things will be given you as well. So do not worry about tomorrow: tomorrow will take care of itself. Each day has enough trouble of its own (Mt. 6:31–34).

A prayer for all seasons. A deep desire for a new heart.

And so, say to the House of Israel, "The Lord Yahweh says this: I am not doing this for your sake, House of Israel, but for the sake of my holy name, which you have profaned among the nations where you have gone. I mean to display the holiness of my great name, which has been profaned among the nations, which you have profaned among them. And the nations will learn that I am Yahweh — it is the Lord Yahweh who speaks — when I display my holiness for your sake before their eyes. Then I am going to take you from among the nations and gather you together from all the foreign countries, and bring you home to your own land. I shall pour clean water over you and you will be cleansed; I shall cleanse you of all your defilement and all your idols. I shall give you a new heart, and put a new spirit in you; I shall remove the heart of stone from your bodies and give you a heart of flesh instead. I shall put my spirit in you, and make you keep my laws and sincerely respect my observances. You will live in the land which I gave your ancestors. You shall be my people and I will be your God" (Ez. 36:22–28).

Worship

We pray that we might be possessed by the Lord:

God our Father, may all nations and peoples praise you. May Jesus, who is called faithful and true and who lives with you eternally, possess our hearts for ever (Daytime Prayer, Saturday, Week I).

Conclusion

A heart love, a total and complete love.

Listen, Israel: Yahweh our God is the one Yahweh. You shall love Yahweh your God with all your heart, with all your soul, with all your strength. Let these words I urge on you today be written on your heart (Dt. 6:4–6).

THIRD HOUR

Theme: Mouth (putting on the mind/words of Christ).
Desire: To speak only truth based on the vision of Jesus.

INTRODUCTION

The highest form of prayer is praise. Prayer focuses more upon God than on anything or anyone else. To truly see God means that we are drawn into praising him. Ask for the Spirit of faith and worship, the Spirit of praise.

Alleluia!

Praise God in his Temple on earth,
praise him in his temple in heaven,
praise him for his mighty achievements,
praise him for his transcendent greatness! (Ps. 150:1).

POINTS

Join Mary in praying to the Father. What did Mary see? Her mind was filled with truth, and her mouth spoke out in song. Let her pray this hymn in your heart.

My soul proclaims the greatness of the Lord
and my spirit exults in God my savior;
because he has looked upon his lowly handmaid.
Yes, from this day forward all generations will call me blessed,
for the Almighty has done great things for me.
Holy is his name,
and his mercy reaches from age to age for those who fear him.
He has shown the power of his arm,
he has routed the proud of heart.

He has pulled down princes from their thrones and exalted the
  lowly.
The hungry he has filled with good things, the rich sent empty
  away.
He has come to the help of Israel his servant, mindful of his
  mercy
—according to the promise he made to our ancestors—
of his mercy to Abraham and to his descendants for ever
(Lk. 1:46–55).

*Wait in silence and then allow Paul to speak. Jesus continues to live
through the "mouth" of Paul. He continues to live when we speak the
truth of God's love and forgiveness.*

Paul stood up, held up a hand for silence and began to speak:
"Men of Israel, and fearers of God, listen! The God of our nation
Israel chose our ancestors, and made our people great when they
were living as foreigners in Egypt; then by divine power he led
them out, and for about forty years took care of them in the
wilderness. When he had destroyed seven nations in Canaan, he
put them in possession of their land for about four hundred and
fifty years. After this he gave judges, down to the prophet
Samuel. Then they demanded a king, and God gave them Saul
son of Kish, a man of the tribe of Benjamin. After forty years, he
deposed him and made David their king, of whom he approved in
these words, 'I have selected David son of Jesse, a man after my
own heart, who will carry out my whole purpose.' To keep his
promise, God has raised up for Israel one of David's descendants,
Jesus, as Savior, whose coming was heralded by John when he
proclaimed a baptism of repentance for the whole people of
Israel. Before John ended his career he said, 'I am not the one you
imagine me to be; that one is coming after me and I am not fit to
undo his sandal'" (Acts 13:16–25).

Worship
With our mouth we pray:

Heavenly Father and God of mercy,
we no longer look for Jesus among the dead,
for he is alive and has become the Lord of life.
From the waters of death you raise us with him
and renew your gift of life within us.
Increase in our minds and hearts

the risen life we share with Christ
and help us to grow as your people
toward the fullness of eternal life with you.
We ask this through Christ our Lord. Amen.
(Evening Prayer II, Sunday within Octave of Easter)

CONCLUSION
The psalmist verbalizes for us a song of praise:

Your love is better than life itself,
my lips will recite your praise;
all my life I will bless you,
in your name lift up my hands;
my soul will feast most richly,
on my lips a song of joy and, in my mouth, praise (Ps.
63:3-5).

FOURTH HOUR

Theme: Hands (doing the work of Christ).
Desire: To incarnate truth and love in action.

INTRODUCTION
The living and true God is the object of prayer — a God of the humble and weak.

Your strength does not lie in numbers,
nor your might in violent men;
since you are the God of the humble,
the help of the oppressed,
the support of the weak,
the refuge of the forsaken,
the savior of the despairing (Jdt. 9:11[16]).

POINTS
Jesus touches the deaf man and brings healing. The gift of touch, of reaching out in love and concern. Our call is to follow in his paths.

Returning from the district of Tyre, he went by way of Sidon toward the Sea of Galilee, right through the Decapolis region. And they brought him a deaf man who had an impediment in his speech; and they asked him to lay his hand on him. He took him aside in private, away from the crowd, put his fingers into the man's ears and touched his tongue with spittle. Then looking up to heaven he sighed; and he said to him, "Ephphatha," that is, "Be opened." And his ears were opened, and the ligament of his tongue was loosened and he spoke clearly. And Jesus ordered them to tell no one about it, but the more he insisted, the more widely they published it. Their admiration was unbounded. "He has done all things well," they said, "he makes the deaf hear and the dumb speak" (Mk. 7:31–37).

The hands of the early Church, busy with assisting those in need and in want. Hands also busy in prayer. Ask the Spirit to enrich our hands.

About this time, when the number of disciples was increasing, the Hellenists made a complaint against the Hebrews: in the daily distribution their own widows were being overlooked. So the Twelve called a full meeting of the disciples and addressed them, "It would not be right for us to neglect the word of God so as to give out food; you, brothers, must select from among yourselves seven men of good reputation, filled with the Spirit and with wisdom; we will hand over this duty to them, and continue to devote ourselves to prayer and to the service of the word." The whole assembly approved of this proposal and elected Stephen, a man full of faith and of the Holy Spirit, together with Philip, Prochorus, Nicanor, Timon, Parmenas, and Nicolaus of Antioch, a convert to Judaism. They presented these to the apostles, who prayed and laid their hands on them (Acts 6:1–6).

WORSHIP

We pray with the Church on the feast of Saint Joseph the Worker:

God our Father,
creator and ruler of the universe,
in every age you call man
to develop and use his gifts for the good of others.
With Saint Joseph as our example and guide,
help us to do the work you have asked
and come to the rewards you have promised.

CONCLUSION
They are happy who walk in the Lord's way and do his work.

Happy, all those who fear Yahweh
   and follow in his paths.
You will eat what your hands have worked for,
   happiness and prosperity will be yours (Ps. 128:1-2).

Day of Trust in God's Gifts

"With faith, with hope, with charity"

FIRST HOUR

Theme: Faith.
Desire: To be taken by the hand.

INTRODUCTION

Prayer is based on faith that God is present here and now and wants to share his life with us. In the darkness we believe. In waiting and silence is our peace.

> Come, let us return to Yahweh.
> He has torn us to pieces, but he will heal us;
> he has struck us down, but he will bandage our wounds;
> after a day or two he will bring us back to life,
> on the third day he will raise us
> and we shall live in his presence (Hos. 6:1–3).

POINTS

Faith is no small feat. Thomas is everyman: demanding evidence before commitment. Happy are those who believe without seeing. Ask for the Spirit of faith.

Thomas, called the Twin, who was one of the Twelve, was not with them when Jesus came. When the disciples said, "We have seen the Lord," he answered, "Unless I see the holes that the nails made in his hands and can put my finger into the holes they made, and unless I can put my hand into his side, I refuse to believe." Eight days later the disciples were in the house again and Thomas was with them. The doors were closed, but Jesus came in and stood among them. "Peace be with you," he said. Then he spoke to Thomas, "Put your finger here; look, here are my hands. Give me your hand; put it into my side. Doubt no longer but believe."

Thomas replied, "My Lord and my God!"

Jesus said to him: "You believe because you can see me. Happy are those who have not seen and yet believe" (Jn. 20:24-29)

The father of faith — to be taken by the hand right up to and through death. We too must go on a trust walk, being led without seeing.

It happened some time later that God put Abraham to the test. "Abraham, Abraham," he called.

"Here I am," he replied.

"Take your son," God said, "your only child Isaac, whom you love, and go to the land of Moriah. There you shall offer him as a burnt offering, on a mountain I will point out to you."

Rising early next morning Abraham saddled his ass and took with him two of his servants and his son Isaac. He chopped wood for the burnt offering and started on his journey to the place God had pointed out to him. On the third day Abraham looked up and saw the place in the distance. Then Abraham said to his servants, "Stay here with the donkey. The boy and I will go over there; we will worship and come back to you" (Gen. 22:1-5).

WORSHIP
We pray for faith:

Lord Jesus Christ, shepherd of your Church, in order to strengthen our faith and to lead us to the kingdom, you renewed and far surpassed the marvels of the old law. Through the uncertainties of this earthly journey, lead us home to the everlasting pastures (Daytime Prayer, Thursday, Week III).

CONCLUSION

Paul calls us to faith. Be grateful for the gift.

The word, that is the faith we proclaim, is very near to you, it is on your lips and in your heart. If your lips confess that Jesus is Lord and if you believe in your heart that God raised him from the dead, then you will be saved. By believing from the heart you are made righteous; by confessing with your lips you are saved (Rom. 10:8b–10).

SECOND HOUR

Theme: Hope.
Desire: To trust in God's ways as we venture into the future.

INTRODUCTION

God's covenant makes prayer possible. He shelters us in his heart and there speaks to us in silent music — "In perfect silence there is music" (Sandburg). Indeed, "be still and know that I am God" (Ps. 46:10).

Look after me, God, I take shelter in you (Ps. 16:1).

POINTS

Hope deals with fear and death. By trusting in Jesus we are saved from the storms of life, both internal and external. Ask for the Spirit of hope — sheer grace.

That evening the disciples went down to the shore of the lake and got into a boat to make for Capernaum on the other side of the lake. It was getting dark by now and Jesus had still not rejoined them. The wind was strong, and the sea was getting rough. They had rowed three or four miles when they saw Jesus walking on the lake and coming towards the boat. This frightened them, but he said, "It is I. Do not be afraid." They were for taking him into the boat, but in no time it reached the shore at the place they were making for (Jn. 6:16–21).

Here is a call to Christian living. Patience is at the heart of hope. By living in Jesus we come to have confidence in what the Lord will do with our lives.

Blessed be God the Father of our Lord Jesus Christ, who in his great mercy has given us a new birth as his sons, by raising Jesus Christ from the dead, so that we have a sure hope and the promise of an inheritance that can never be spoilt or soiled and never fade away, because it is being kept for you in the heavens. Through your faith, God's power will guard you until the salvation which has been prepared is revealed at the end of time. This is a cause of great joy for you, even though you may for a short time have to bear being plagued by all sorts of trials; so that, when Jesus Christ is revealed, your faith will have been tested and proved like gold — only it is more precious than gold, which is corruptible even though it bears testing by fire — and then you will have praise and glory and honor. You did not see him, yet you love him; and still without seeing him, you are already filled with a joy so glorious that it cannot be described, because you believe; and you are sure of the end to which your faith looks forward, that is, the salvation of your souls (1 Pet. 1:3-9).

WORSHIP
We pray for hope:

Father of our Lord Jesus Christ,
ever faithful to your promises
and ever close to your Church:
the earth rejoices in hope of the Savior's coming
and looks forward with longing
to his return at the end of time.
(Office of Readings, 3rd Sunday of Advent)

CONCLUSION
A letter sent to us all.

From Paul, servant of God, an apostle of Jesus Christ to bring those whom God has chosen to faith and to the knowledge of the truth that leads to true religion; and to give them the hope of the eternal life that was promised so long ago by God (1 Tit. 1:1).

THIRD HOUR

Theme: Charity.
Desire: To ground and root our lives in love.

INTRODUCTION

Prayer involves opening our door to the Lord. We must hear his call and realize how he longs to share our meal with us. What love God has for us! Praise him!

> Look, I am standing at the door, knocking. If one of you hears me calling and opens the door, I will come in to share his meal, side by side with him (Rev. 3:20).

POINTS

"Jesus looked steadily at him and loved him" — God gazes at us with the same love. Does our "richness" block us from receiving that love and then causing a deep sadness?

> He was setting out on a journey when a man ran up, knelt before him and put this question to him, "Good master, what must I do to inherit eternal life?"
> Jesus said to him, "Why do you call me good? No one is good but God alone. You know the commandments: You must not kill; You must not commit adultery; Honor your father and mother."
> And he said to him, "Master, I have kept all these from my earliest days."
> Jesus looked steadily at him and loved him, and he said, "There is one thing you lack. Go and sell everything you own and give the money to the poor, and you will have treasure in heaven; then come, follow me." But his face fell at these words and he went away sad, for he was a man of great wealth (Mk. 10:17-22).

Go through the list and examine your life. Love is a spiritual gift given in grace. We must ask for the Spirit of love, the greatest gift of all.

> Love is always patient and kind; it is never jealous; love is never boastful or conceited; it is never rude or selfish; it does not take offense, and is not resentful. Love takes no pleasure in other people's sins but delights in the truth; it is always ready to excuse, to trust, to hope, and to endure whatever comes (1 Cor. 13:4-7).

WORSHIP
An evening prayer:

Merciful Lord,
let the evening prayer of your Church
come before you.
May we do your work faithfully;
free us from sin
and make us secure in your love.
(Evening Prayer, Wednesday, Week III)

CONCLUSION
Ponder these words. What mystery! What grace!

We ourselves have known and put our faith in
God's love toward ourselves.
God is love
and anyone who lives in love lives in God,
and God lives in him (1 Jn. 4:16).

FOURTH HOUR

Theme: Integration (holiness is wholeness).
Desire: To integrate the human and divine in our lives.

INTRODUCTION
Prayer leads to the doing of God's will. We need wisdom for this: to know what is truly pleasing in God's sight. Ask for the gift of discerning what is and what is not of God's mind and heart.

With you is Wisdom, she who knows your works,
she who was present when you made the world;
she understands what is pleasing in your eyes
and what agrees with your commandments (Wis. 9:9).

POINTS
Soundness demands both inner and outer integrity. Jesus' words are

strong in calling us to being total persons. He gives us not only the challenge but the grace as well.

He also told a parable to them, "Can one blind man guide another? Surely both will fall into a pit? The disciple is not superior to his teacher; the fully trained disciple will always be like his teacher. Why do you observe the splinter in your brother's eye and never notice the plank in your own? How can you say to your brother, 'Brother, let me take out the splinter that is in your eye,' when you cannot see the plank in your own? Hypocrite! Take the plank out of your own eye first, and then you will see clearly enough to take out the splinter that is in your brother's eye.

"There is no sound tree that produces rotten fruit, nor again a rotten tree that produces sound fruit. For every tree can be told by its own fruit: people do not pick figs from thorns, nor gather grapes from brambles. A good man draws what is good from the store of goodness in his heart; a bad man draws what is bad from the store of badness. For a man's words flow out of what fills his heart" (Lk. 6:39–45).

Jesus is our model of wholeness. He lived in the Father's presence and had singleness of vision. Grace enriches us in faith, hope, and charity, making us whole and holy.

Men of Israel, listen to what I am going to say: Jesus the Nazarene was a man commended to you by God by the miracles and portents and signs that God worked through him when he was among you, as you all know. This man, who was put into your power by the deliberate intention and foreknowledge of God, you took and crucified by men outside the Law. You killed him, but God raised him to life, freeing him from the pangs of Hades; for it was impossible for him to be held in its power since, as David says of him:
> I saw the Lord before me always,
> for with him at my right hand nothing can shake me.
> So my heart was glad
> and my tongue cried out with joy;
> my body, too, will rest in the hope
> that you will not abandon my soul to Hades
> nor allow your holy one to experience corruption.
> You have made known the way of life to me,
> you will fill me with gladness through your presence (Acts 2:22–28).

WORSHIP

Prayer for integrity:

> Father, he who knew no sin was made sin for us, to save us and
> restore us to your friendship. Look upon our contrite heart and
> afflicted spirit and heal our troubled conscience, so that in the joy
> and strength of the Holy Spirit we may proclaim your praise and
> glory before all the nations (Morning Prayer, Friday, Week III).

CONCLUSION

God's presence: goal and source of our integration.

> You will reveal the path of life to me,
> give me unbounded joy in your presence,
> and at your right hand everlasting pleasures (Ps. 16:11).

Day of Companionship with the Lord

"That I may run, rise, rest with thee"

FIRST HOUR

Theme: Running with the Lord.
Desire: To live through love in his presence.

INTRODUCTION

God is with us and for us. In prayer we experience his nearness and love. Paul expresses the core of our Christian life: living, loving, being with.

> Before the world was made, he chose us, chose us in Christ,
> to be holy and spotless, and to live through love in his
>   presence,
> determining that we should become his adopted sons, through
>   Jesus Christ
> for his own kind purposes,
> to make us praise the glory of his grace,
> his free gift to us in the Beloved,
> in whom, through his blood, we gain our freedom, the
>   forgiveness of our sins (Eph. 1:4–7).

Points

The disciples walk (run interiorly) with the Lord. We are all pilgrims seeking our way. We pray that the Lord will be our guide.

When they drew near to the village to which they were going, he made as if to go on; but they pressed him to stay with them. "It is nearly evening," they said, "and the day is almost over." So he went in to stay with them. Now while he was with them at table, he took the bread and said the blessing; then he broke it and handed it to them. And their eyes were opened and they recognized him; but he had vanished from their sight. Then they said to each other, "Did not our hearts burn within us as he talked to us on the road and explained the scriptures to us?"

They set out that instant and returned to Jerusalem. There they found the Eleven assembled together with their companions, who said to them, "Yes, it is true. The Lord has risen and has appeared to Simon." Then they told their story of what had happened on the road and how they had recognized him at the breaking of bread (Lk. 24:28–35).

Here the disciples actually run in their searching for the Lord. He is already in their hearts as they look outside for his presence. Jesus dwells within us; he runs with us all the days of our life.

It was very early on the first day of the week and still dark when Mary of Magdala came to the tomb. She saw that the stone had been moved away from the tomb and came running to Simon Peter and the other disciple, the one Jesus loved. "They have taken the Lord out of the tomb," she said, "and we don't know where they have put him."

So Peter set out with the other disciple to go to the tomb. They ran together but the other disciple, running faster than Peter, reached the tomb first; he bent down and saw the linen cloths lying on the ground, but did not go in. Simon Peter who was following now came up, went right into the tomb, saw the linen cloths on the ground, and also the cloth that had been over his head; this was not with the linen cloths but rolled up in a place by itself. Then the other disciple who had reached the tomb first also went in; he saw and he believed. Till this moment they had failed to understand the teaching of scripture, that he must rise from the dead. The disciples then went home again (Jn. 20:1–10).

WORSHIP

We pray:

God of mercy,
you gave us saints to proclaim
  the riches of Christ.
By the help of their prayers
may we grow in knowledge of you,
be eager to do good,
and learn to walk before you
by living the truth of the gospel.
(Common of Pastors)

CONCLUSION

What happens when we run with and for the Lord?

As for me, my life is already being poured away as a libation, and the time has come for me to be gone. I have fought the good fight to the end; I have run the race to the finish; I have kept the faith; all there is to come now is the crown of righteousness reserved for me, which the Lord, the righteous judge, will give to me on that Day; and not only to me but to all those who have longed for his appearing (2 Tim. 4:6–8).

SECOND HOUR

Theme: Rising with the Lord (new beginnings).
Desire: To start every activity in the Lord.

INTRODUCTION

Who has the right to enter the tent of God? Yet, in prayer we are invited to sit with the Lord and then to rise with him in doing his will. Ask for the grace to start this prayer and every activity in the Lord.

Yahweh, who has the right to enter your tent,
or to live on your holy mountain?
The man whose way of life is blameless,
who always does what is right,

who speaks the truth from his heart,
whose tongue is not used for slander (Ps. 15:1-2).

POINTS

With reverence, witness what happens here. What went on in the heart of the leper? In being cured how he was raised up to new life. What deep gratitude! Now all was new and different!

> After he had come down from the mountain large crowds followed him. A leper now came up and bowed low in front of him. "Sir," he said, "if you want to, you can cure me." Jesus stretched out his hand, touched him and said, "Of course I want to! Be cured!" And his leprosy was cured at once. Then Jesus said to him, "Mind you do not tell anyone, but go and show yourself to the priest and make the offering prescribed by Moses, as evidence for them" (Mt. 8:1-4).

Paul explains how we were brought back to life (raised up). Now our life is hidden in Christ. We rise and work in and through him. Great intimacy here.

> Since you have been brought back to true life with Christ, you must look for the things that are in heaven, where Christ is, sitting at God's right hand. Let your thoughts be on heavenly things, not on the things that are on the earth, because you have died, and now the life you have is hidden with Christ in God. But when Christ is revealed—and he is your life—you too will be revealed in all your glory with him (Col. 3:1-4).

WORSHIP

A traditional prayer:

> Direct, we beseech thee, O Lord, our actions by thy holy inspiration, and carry them on by thy gracious assistance that every prayer and work of ours may begin always from thee and through thee be happily ended.

CONCLUSION

A call to rise at night to praise our God and dwell in his presence.

Have I not said, Yahweh, that my task
is to observe your words?
Wholeheartedly I now entreat you,

take pity on me as you have promised!
After reflecting on my behavior,
  I turn my feet to your decrees.
Wasting no time, I hurry
  to observe your commandments.
Though the nooses of the wicked tighten round me,
  I do not forget your Law.
I get up at midnight to thank you
  for the righteousness of your rulings.
I am a friend of all who fear you
  and observe your precepts.
Yahweh, your love fills the earth:
  teach me your statutes (Ps. 119:57–64).

THIRD HOUR

Theme: Resting in the Lord.
Desire: To conclude all things in the Lord.

Introduction

Prayer is like the desert; we leave all things and all people behind to be alone with our God. Here, and only here, do we truly rest. Nothing other than the Lord can truly satisfy our hearts. Peace is to be one with God.

And I say,
"Oh for the wings of a dove
  to fly away and find rest."
How far I would take my flight,
  and make a new home in the desert!
There I should soon find shelter
  from the raging wind,
and from the tempest, Lord, that destroys,
  and from their malicious tongues (Ps. 55:6–9).

Points

The gentle invitation to come to the Lord and find our rest in him. Retreat as vacation time! No work — just being with.

Come to me, all you who labor and are overburdened, and I will give you rest. Shoulder my yoke and learn from me, for I am gentle and humble in heart, and you will find rest for your souls. Yes, my yoke is easy and my burden light (Mt. 11:28–30).

In the covenant that God offers us do we find our rest and our home. It is a covenant of the heart. In silence and surrender, God teaches us all things.

See, the days are coming – it is Yahweh who speaks – when I will make a new covenant with the House of Israel (and the House of Judah), but not a covenant like the one I made with their ancestors on the day I took them by the hand to bring them out of the land of Egypt. They broke that covenant of mine, so I had to show them who was master. It is Yahweh who speaks. No, this is the covenant I will make with the House of Israel when those days arrive – it is Yahweh who speaks. Deep within them I will plant my Law, writing it on their hearts. Then I will be their God and they shall be my people. There will be no further need for neighbor to try to teach neighbor, or brother to say to brother, "Learn to know Yahweh!" No, they will all know me, the least no less than the greatest – it is Yahweh who speaks – since I will forgive their iniquity and never call their sin to mind (Jer. 31:31–34).

WORSHIP
A prayer from the Easter season:

Lord,
we have celebrated today
the mystery of the rising of Christ
    to new life.
May we now rest in your peace,
safe from all that could harm us,
and rise again refreshed and joyful,
to praise you throughout another day.
(Night Prayer, Sunday)

CONCLUSION
Resting in the Lord brings peace, his gift to us.

I am listening. What is Yahweh saying?
What God is saying means peace
for his people, for his friends,

if only they renounce their folly;
for those who fear him, his saving help is near,
and the glory will then live in our country (Ps. 85:8-9).

FOURTH HOUR

Theme: Fellowship.
Desire: To share our whole life with God.

Introduction

As Paul journeyed with Christ, so Tychicus is a companion of Paul. Prayer is a time of deep companionship (cum = with; panis = bread), a time to break bread together. Prayer is a sharing of lives and loves.

Tychicus will tell you all the news about me. He is a brother I love very much, and a loyal helper and companion in the service of the Lord. I am sending him to you precisely for this purpose: to give you news about us and reassure you (Col. 4:7-8).

Points

Breakfast with the Lord. In sharing food we symbolically share all of our life. All things come together at the meal, at the Eucharist.

As soon as they came ashore they saw that there was some bread there, and a charcoal fire with fish cooking on it. Jesus said, "Bring some of the fish you have just caught." Simon Peter went aboard and dragged the net to the shore, full of big fish, one hundred and fifty-three of them; and in spite of there being so many the net was not broken.
Jesus said to them, "Come and have breakfast."
None of the disciples was bold enough to ask, "Who are you?"; they knew quite well it was the Lord. Jesus then stepped forward, took the bread and gave it to them, and the same with the fish. This was the third time that Jesus showed himself to the disciples after rising from the dead (Jn. 21:9-14).

Paul reveals his deep fellowship in the Lord. Through faith their lives are one. Our lives are to be lived in deep union with Christ Jesus.

Though we were born Jews and not pagan sinners, we acknowledge that what makes a man righteous is not obedience to the Law, but faith in Jesus Christ. We had to become believers in Christ Jesus no less than you had, and now we hold that faith in Christ rather than fidelity to the Law is what justifies us, and that no one can be justified by keeping the Law. Now if we were to admit that the result of looking to Christ to justify us is to make us sinners like the rest, it would follow that Christ had induced us to sin, which would be absurd. If I were to return to a position I had already abandoned, I should be dead to the Law, so that now I can live for God. I have been crucified with Christ, and I live now not with my own life but with the life of Christ who lives in me. The life I now live in this body I live in faith: faith in the Son of God who loved me and who sacrificed himself for my sake. I cannot bring myself to give up God's gift: if the Law can justify us, there is no point in the death of Christ (Gal. 2:15–21).

WORSHIP
With the Church we pray:

Heavenly Father and God of mercy,
we no longer look for Jesus among the dead,
for he is alive and has become the Lord of life.
From the waters of death you raise us with him
and renew your gift of life within us.
Increase in our minds and hearts
the risen life we share with Christ
and help us to grow as your people
toward the fullness of eternal life with you.
(Second Sunday of Easter)

CONCLUSION
Deep companionship here: unity and peace.

Hard-pressed, I invoked Yahweh,
 he heard me and came to my relief.
With Yahweh on my side, I fear nothing:
 what can man do to me?
With Yahweh on my side, best help of all,
 I can triumph over my enemies (Ps. 118:5–7).

Day of Praise for Who God Is
and for What He Has Done
and Is Doing
"Trinity Sunday"

FIRST HOUR

Theme: God our Father.
Desire: To know the Father of our Lord Jesus Christ.

INTRODUCTION

The focus of prayer is God. With loving attention we strive to rest in his presence and listen in silence to his word. Only the Spirit can reveal to us the true nature of who our Father is. Beg for that Spirit.

> Blessed be God the Father of our Lord Jesus Christ, who has blessed us with all the spiritual blessings of heaven in Christ (Eph. 1:3).

POINTS

Listen as Jesus prays to the Father. Ask Jesus to allow you to come to an ever deeper knowledge of who his Father is. We come into the presence of mystery.

At that time Jesus exclaimed, "I bless you, Father, Lord of heaven and of earth, for hiding these things from the learned and the clever and revealing them to mere children. Yes, Father, for that is what it pleased you to do. Everything has been entrusted to me by my Father; and no one knows the Son except the Father, just as no one knows the Father except the Son and those to whom the Son chooses to reveal him" (Mt. 11:25–27).

God our Father is love. We come to know him as he is when we truly love him and our neighbor. The Father is totally simple — pure light.

My dear people,
let us love one another
since love comes from God
and everyone who loves is begotten by God and knows God.
Anyone who fails to love can never have known God,
because God is love.

God's love for us was revealed
when God sent into the world his only Son
so that we could have life through him;
this is the love I mean:
not our love for God,
but God's love for us when he sent his Son
to be the sacrifice that takes our sins away.

My dear people,
since God has loved us so much,
we too should love one another.
No one has ever seen God;
but as long as we love one another
God will live in us
because he lets us share his Spirit.
We ourselves saw and we testify
that the Father sent his Son
as savior of the world.
If anyone acknowledges that Jesus is the Son of God,
God lives in him, and he in God.
We ourselves have known and put our faith in
God's love toward ourselves.

God is love
and anyone who lives in love lives in God
and God lives in him (1 Jn. 4:7–16).

Worship
A prayer from Trinity Sunday:

Father,
you sent your Word to bring us truth
and your Spirit to make us holy.
Through them we come to know the mystery
   of your life.
Help us to worship you, one God in three Persons,
by proclaiming and living our faith in you.

Conclusion
The Father's name is great and to be honored.

Yahweh, our Lord,
how great your name throughout the earth! (Ps. 8:1).

SECOND HOUR

Theme: Jesus Christ, the Son of God.
Desire: To know the Lord Jesus.

Introduction
Our journey to the Father is in Jesus. In prayer, we go through Jesus to the Father. In silence we must allow the Father to show us what his Son is like.

That is why all you who are holy brothers and have had the same heavenly call should turn your minds to Jesus, the apostle and the high priest of our religion. He was faithful to the one who appointed him, just like Moses, who stayed faithful in all his house; but he has been found to deserve a greater glory than Moses (Heb. 3:1-3).

Points
Jesus, through John's Gospel, tells us who he is. Enter into the mystery of this revelation and allow your heart to be touched by so gracious and caring a Lord. Jesus is a giver of life.

"I tell you most solemnly, anyone who does not enter the sheepfold through the gate, but gets in some other way is a thief and a
brigand. The one who enters through the gate is the shepherd of
the flock; the gatekeeper lets him in, the sheep hear his voice, one
by one he calls his own sheep and leads them out. When he has
brought out his flock, he goes ahead of them, and the sheep
follow because they know his voice. They never follow a stranger
but run away from him: they do not recognize the voice of
strangers."

Jesus told them this parable but they failed to understand what
he meant by telling it to them.

So Jesus spoke to them again:

"I tell you most solemnly,
I am the gate of the sheepfold.
All others who have come
are thieves and brigands;
but the sheep took no notice of them.
I am the gate.

Anyone who enters through me will be safe:
he will go freely in and out
and be sure of finding pasture.
The thief comes
only to steal and kill and destroy.
I have come
so that they may have life
and have it to the full" (Jn. 10:1-10).

*Paul's deep desire to know Jesus. That knowledge is gained through
suffering, by accepting the cross. Ponder this mystery; enter into it.*

But because of Christ, I have come to consider all these advan-
tages that I had as disadvantages. Not only that, but I believe
nothing can happen that will outweigh the supreme advantage of
knowing Christ Jesus my Lord. For him I have accepted the loss
of everything, and I look on everything as so much rubbish if
only I can have Christ, and be given a place in him. I am no
longer trying for perfection by my own efforts, the perfection
that comes from the Law, but I want only the perfection that
comes through faith in Christ, and is from God and based on
faith. All I want is to know Christ and the power of his resurrection and to share his sufferings by reproducing the pattern of his
death. That is the way I can hope to take my place in the resurrection of the dead (Phil. 3:7-11).

Worship
We pray:

> God, we praise you:
> Father all-powerful, Christ Lord and Savior,
>   Spirit of love.
> You reveal yourself in the depths of our being,
> drawing us to share in your life and your love.
> One God, three Persons,
> be near to the people formed in your image,
> close to the world your love brings to life.
> (Trinity Sunday)

Conclusion
Jesus reveals the Father to us.

> He is the image of the unseen God
> and the first-born of all creation,
> for in him were created
> all things in heaven and on earth:
> everything visible and everything invisible,
> Thrones, Dominations, Sovereignties, Powers —
> all things were created through him and for him (Col.
> 1:15-16).

THIRD HOUR

Theme: God the Holy Spirit.
Desire: To be open to the Spirit throughout our lives.

Introduction
In our weakness, the Spirit takes our prayer to the Father through Jesus. What a gift! We must open our hearts to be moved by the Spirit of the Father and of the Son.

The Spirit too comes to help us in our weakness. For when we cannot choose words in order to pray properly, the Spirit himself expresses our plea in a way that could never be put into words, and God who knows everything in our hearts knows perfectly well what he means, and that the pleas of the saints expressed by the Spirit are according to the mind of God (Rom. 8:26–27).

POINTS

Enter into this situation. What is the Spirit of Jesus like? That same Spirit calls us to follow the example of our Lord.

He came to Nazara, where he had been brought up, and went into the synagogue on the sabbath day as he usually did. He stood up to read, and they handed him the scroll of the prophet Isaiah. Unrolling the scroll he found the place where it is written:
The spirit of the Lord has been given to me,
for he has anointed me.
He has sent me to bring the good news to the poor,
to proclaim liberty to captives
and to the blind new sight,
to set the downtrodden free,
to proclaim the Lord's year of favor (Lk. 4:16–19).

Paul spells out in specifics the signs of the Spirit of God and the signs of the spirit that are not of the Father and Jesus. The Spirit is not vague, but almost too clear.

Let me put it like this: if you are guided by the Spirit you will be in no danger of yielding to self-indulgence, since self-indulgence is the opposite of the Spirit, the Spirit is totally against such a thing, and it is precisely because the two are so opposed that you do not always carry out your good intentions. If you are led by the Spirit, no law can touch you. When self-indulgence is at work the results are obvious: fornication, gross indecency and sexual irresponsibility; idolatry and sorcery; feuds and wrangling, jealousy, bad temper and quarrels; disagreements, factions, envy; drunkenness, orgies and similar things. I warn you now, as I warned you before: those who behave like this will not inherit the kingdom of God. What the Spirit brings is very different: love, joy, peace, patience, kindness, goodness, trustfulness, gentleness and self-control. There can be no law against things like that, of course. You cannot belong to Christ Jesus unless you crucify all self-indulgent passions and desires.
Since the Spirit is our life, let us be directed by the Spirit. We

must stop being conceited, provocative and envious (Gal. 5:16–26).

Worship
An Easter prayer:

Almighty and ever-living God,
you fulfilled the Easter promise
by sending us your Holy Spirit.
May that Spirit unite the races and nations
    on earth
to proclaim your glory.
(Office of Readings, Pentecost)

Conclusion
The Spirit at work in the early Church.

They were all filled with the Holy Spirit, and began to speak foreign languages as the Spirit gave them the gift of speech (Acts 2:4).

FOURTH HOUR

Theme: The paschal mystery.
Desire: To live, die, and rise with Jesus.

Introduction
Prayer helps us to put things in order. Jesus is our shepherd and Lord. If we have him, we lack nothing.

Yahweh is my shepherd,
    I lack nothing (Ps. 23:1).

Points
Our Christian lives imitate the life of Jesus: doing the Father's will, dying for others, rising to new life. The Gospel tells us of this journey.

From the sixth hour there was darkness over all the land until the ninth hour. And about the ninth hour, Jesus cried out in a loud voice, "Eli, Eli, lama sabachthani?" that is, "My God, my God, why have you deserted me?"

When some of those who stood there heard this, they said, "The man is calling on Elijah," and one of them quickly ran to get a sponge which he dipped in vinegar and, putting it on a reed, gave it him to drink. "Wait!" said the rest of them, "and see if Elijah will come to save him." But Jesus, again crying out in a loud voice, yielded up his spirit.

At that, the veil of the Temple was torn in two from top to bottom; the earth quaked; the rocks were split; the tombs opened and the bodies of many holy men rose from the dead, and these, after his resurrection, came out of the tombs, entered the Holy City and appeared to a number of people. Meanwhile the centurion, together with the others guarding Jesus, had seen the earthquake and all that was taking place, and they were terrified and said, "In truth this was a son of God."

And many women were there, watching from a distance, the same women who had followed Jesus from Galilee and looked after him. Among them were Mary of Magdala, Mary the mother of James and Joseph, and the mother of Zebedee's sons (Mt. 27:45-56).

Paul calls us to put on the mind and heart of Jesus. In doing this, we find true happiness and meaning. Christian life is both cross and crown, death and life.

If our life in Christ means anything to you, if love can persuade at all, or the Spirit that we have in common, or any tenderness and sympathy, then be united in your convictions and united in your love, with a common purpose and a common mind. That is the one thing which would make me completely happy. There must be no competition among you, no conceit; but everybody is to be self-effacing. Always consider the other person to be better than yourself, so that nobody thinks of his own interests first but everybody thinks of other people's interests instead. In your minds you must be the same as Christ Jesus:

> His state was divine,
> yet he did not cling
> to his equality with God
> but emptied himself
> to assume the condition of a slave,
> and became as men are;
> and being as all men are,
> he was humbler yet,

       even to accepting death,
       death on a cross.
       But God raised him high
       and gave him the name
       which is above all other names
       so that all beings
       in the heavens, on earth and in the underworld,
       should bend the knee at the name of Jesus
       and that every tongue should acclaim
       Jesus Christ as Lord,
       to the glory of God the Father (Phil. 2:1-11).

WORSHIP

We pray:

Lord Jesus Christ, you were made obedient unto death, and your name was exalted above all others. Teach us always to do the Father's will, so that, made holy by obedience which unites us to the sacrifice of your body, we can expect your great love in times of sorrow and sing a new song to our God (Daytime Prayer, Monday, Week II).

CONCLUSION

A dwelling with our triune God.

If anyone loves me he will keep my word,
and my Father will love him,
and we shall come to him
and make our home with him (Jn. 14:23).